Toni Morrison

# Toni Morrison

## LITERARY PERSPECTIVES AND CRITICAL INTERPRETATIONS

Editors

DR AJIT KUMAR AND DR RAFSEENA M

Vitasta

Published by
Renu Kaul Verma
Vitasta Publishing Pvt Ltd
2/15, Ansari Road, Daryaganj
New Delhi-110 002
info@vitastapublishing.com

ISBN 978-81-960413-8-0

First Edition 2023

MRP ₹ 495



Edited by Mehnaz Hussain
Cover and Layout by Somesh Kumar Mishra
Printed by Chaman Enterprises, New Delhi

# CONTENTS

**SECTION FIVE**

**Pain, Pleasure and Existentialism**

# FOREWORD

> "There is really nothing more to say—except why. But since why is difficult to handle, one must take refuge in how."
>
> —*The Bluest Eye*

IN THE still, dark silence of early morning, roosters *singaut* (sing out) as if they are calling the sun to wake up the entire village and begin the day. The morning coolness of the mountains meets the sounds of axes and bush knives breaking wood to replenish the fires as women and girls blow steady long breaths onto embers from the previous night's fires. From *ol haus lain* (small groupings of grass and woven bamboo homes) the laughter of children and quiet *tok i go kam* (conversations) are heard. The melody of human voices moves through the villages and fades as *ol go long gaden bilong em* (all go to their gardens). The morning progresses and the village turns quiet, except for the occasional animal rustling through the rain forest, children playing as they meander through the day's adventures, or the men escaping work to play cards. At midday, the season being dry, brings winds swooshing around and through the woven houses, while *taim bilong ren* (the rainy season) drops sheets of rain that block out all but the closest sounds. As the sun lowers, the symphony of village sounds rise as *ol manmeri* (people) return to the *haus lain* to prepare food and *tok stori* (tell stories) around the fire. This is the place, where I began reading Toni Morrison in The Highlands of Papua New Guinea, the Okapa District.

As a Peace Corps volunteer in the later part of the 20th century, this is where I learned the trade language *Melanesian Tok Pisin*, lived in the rainforest with the South Foré people, and focused on developmental work in six villages—*Kamila, Nosuguri, Ponamandi, Takai-Purosa, Ilasa, and Awarosa*. The South Foré are generous people living in a bountiful place, except for the years they had experienced severe drought. Tribes farmed on their own lands, and families harvested coffee for income. They built their homes from materials provided by nature and supplemented tools and hardware available from shops in the provincial capitol. All this beauty, joy and community was surrounded by and steeped in the legacies of colonization and white supremacy. Papua New Guineans called most White men, not by their names but *Masta* and White women, *Missus*. In my time there, too many expats, primarily white Americans and Australians seemed bolstered by this nomenclature. In this context, when I was read as American, I too became Missus. Blackness was a barrier, especially outside the villages. In the cities, my Blackness prevented me from going into some places and demanded the searching of my person and bags upon leaving stores. Womanhood was being silenced nearly everywhere. It prevented me from being recognized when I spoke and often left me without any platform to speak at all. Such communication barriers continued among women who did not know *Melanesian Tok Pisin*. In this case, school girls and educated women spoke on my behalf and translated for me. Being a citizen of the United States of America, on occasion, allowed me to sidestep these limitations provided I was with other Americans or White people. I became serious about reading Toni Morrison novels in Papua New Guinea—*Sula, Song of Solomon, The Bluest Eye*—and continued this reading as I traveled back to the USA through the South Pacific and Europe. Reading Morrison in these places where my body was subjected to different types of treatment depending on who other people thought I was, allowed me to experience my Blackness, womanhood and her work in ways that helped me to see my home country i.e., the US, the Black diaspora, and womanhood with more complexity.

This thoughtfully curated collection of chapters attends to the body of work Toni Morrison created; particularly its role, influence, contribution, and relevance. Each chapter offers a different take, facet, or angle on Morrison's writings. Some focus on specific works such as *The Bluest Eye, Sula, Beloved, Playing in the Dark, A Mercy,* and *God Help the Child,* and some study Morrison's work in comparison with other authors (Alice Walker, Arundhaati Roy, Khaled Hosseini), and philosophies (Kawaida, Existentialism). Others consider what Morrison makes present in her fiction and non-fiction writing including city images, gender and race, mother and daughter relations, the subaltern, domesticity, and inner furies, as well as the work she does in her writing such as magic realism, re-memory, poly-vocality, multiple narratives, and challenging metanarratives that sidestep Black women's experiences. This is a book on the body of Morrison's work as intellectual property and a quest for self-identity. Reading this work reminded me of my own readings of Morrison in places where the realities of Black women's lives were shaped differently by histories that unfolded across the planet in unique ways solidly unified in colonization, marginalization, and exploitation. Morrison offers a refuge for understanding how these forces are and have been at work. This book *Toni Morrison: Literary Perspectives and Critical Interpretations*

makes space for the 'how' of Morrison.

**—M Francyne Huckaby**
Professor of Curriculum Studies
Associated Dean of School of Interdisciplinary Studies
Texas Christian University, Texas, USA

# INTRODUCTION

## PART I

A TRUE icon and spokesperson of the Black female world, Toni Morrison's legacy remains alive to the core of her distinct African American origin. Her literary oeuvre subscribes her individuality to be counted as one of the strong Black female voices to emerge in the history of African American Literature. Laurels, awards, achievements and recognitions which Morrison received for the immeasurable contributions that her works speak out, undoubtedly has created the air which resonates with the rhythm of time. Born as Chloe Anthony Wofford to George and Rahmah Willis in 1931 in Lorain, Ohio, Toni Morrison was not an exception to the harshness of being a Black woman in America. Her commitment to the African American cause is amply manifested in her works where she vocalizes the Black experiences in succinct terms.

The literary output of Morrison, spanning across three decades, has had its reception as well as criticism; but Morrison's novels tell us tales which she herself wanted to read. With eleven novels to her credit, along with children's books and prose pieces, Morrison's recognition as the first African American woman novelist to win the Nobel Prize in Literature in 1993, rests in the observation that her "novels" are "characterized by visionary force and poetic import" by the Swedish Academy (New York Times "Toni Morrison, Towering Novelist of the Black Experience, Dies at 88").

Serious academic interventions and studies on Toni Morrison's works echo the seriousness with which the literary world had received it. *The Bluest Eye* (1970) which recorded Morrison's career with the breathtaking narration of a black girl being victimized by the viciousness of White standards of beauty, challenges the historical dream of Martin Luther King. While the notion of equality between the African Americans and the Whites stood at an unfathomable distance to be covered the poisonous nature of racism could not be detoxicated using any measures of human rights. Various observations on the novel truly highlight Morrison's efforts to voice 'the reality of violence within the Black community' (Mckay 139).

A different yet bold treatment of queer relationship is what *Sula* (1974) resonated within its pages. Morrison's deft use of the protagonist Sula to cut through the most significant and loveliest aspect of human bonding highlights the essential nature of Black womanhood in purely African American terms. Though the initial reception of Sula's character seemed to make the divide between what is acceptable and what is not, it could be said assertively that Morrison was walking well ahead of her times when she gave us Sula as a distorted version of femininity.

The quest for identity, which is at par with the universal theme across the literary world, forms the central concern in

*Song of Solomon* (1977). Perceived as a narrative which combines 'elements of the bildungsroman and the mystery genre on Milkman's quest to understand his nature, his family, and his place in the world' (Kubitschek 71), Morrison has provided us with the lens to understand how the power dynamics of the dialectical relationship between capitalism, racism and sexism is woven intricately in the lives of the African American community. With Milkman's struggle depicted as having a universal appeal, Morrison sets the *Song of Solomon* as 'the narrative of an individual's self-discovery, an examination of the way gender and class have shaped different versions of African American experience, a rewriting of American history, and a dialogue with literary and cultural genealogies of American, African, and European provenance' (Roynon 28).

Morrison's fourth novel *Tar Baby* (1981), which provided 'a composite picture of America in Black and White' (Samuels and Clenora Hudson-Weems 8), depicted 'class struggle, the struggle between the ruling class and the subject class' (Mbalia 89). The novel focuses on various cultural conflicts which are portrayed through the couples Morrison paints in her narrative. Valerian and Margaret Street—the White couple—reveal the dynamics of the White American sexuality. Sydney and Ondine—the first Black couple—stand as the representatives of all those African Americans who experience various problems in providing education to their children in the Eurocentric context. The third couple—Son and Jadine—'embody the conflict between traditional, rural southern African American culture and a less defined hybrid culture with elements from Africa, America, and Europe' (Mbalia 92). With *Tar Baby*, Morrison not only depicted the conflict between race, class and sex but also developed a narrative space which is "deeply perceptive of a Blackman's desire to create a mythology of his own to replace the stereotypes and myths the white man has constructed for him. It is also a book about a woman's anger and her denial of her need for an impossible man (The New York Times Book Review).

*Beloved*, which was published in 1987, 'depicts a postbellum community of ex-slaves in Cincinnati grappling with the traumatic legacy of slavery as it is embodied in an infant ghost named Beloved, who was murdered by her mother, Sethe, in an effort to save the child from enslavement' (Zamalin 205). Recording the experiences of a slave in bits and pieces, Morrison offers a Black world which is rendered sick with racial violence. Placing the characters Sethe and Denver in the shadow of Beloved, Morrison presents her readers with a narrative which brings forth the evils of the institution of slavery.

Depicting the story of racial violence in *Jazz* (1992), Morrison places its focus on Harlem in the 1920s, throwing light on the disturbed lives of Joe, Violet and Dorcas. The novel, according to Rodrigues in 'Experiencing Jazz,' 'jazzifies the history of a people. Morrison extends the range of her fictional world by giving us rapid and vivid glimpses of their life in the rural South after emancipation' (158).

The third novel in the trilogy, *Paradise* (1997) focuses on presenting a re-interpretation of the significance of the Black community, the importance of tradition as well as the relevance of the concept of home for the Black community in the United States. Set in the fictional town Ruby, the nine Black families who have been travelling from Mississippi to Oklahoma in the hope of joining their ancestors ends up being disallowed by the light skinned African Americans. Being rejected by the people of their own race, the nine African American families establish their own town Ruby which is isolated from the outside world. However, with the passage of time, the people of the town are influenced by the outside wickedness, resulting in the disintegration of the utopian sense attached to the establishment of the town.

Noticed for the polyphonic narrative offered by the female characters in *Love* (2003), Morrison deals with the elusive nature of love delineated through the love relationship which the female characters shared with Bill Cosey, the deceased hotel owner. The novel is about love and betrayal with abandonment seen as the key element in the characterization of Heed, Christine and Junior. Morrison directs her attention to the trauma that these female characters have lived through in their past, and provides the space to look into how the traumatic past has affected their present.

While majority of Morrison's novels focused on the issues related to the African American female characters, *Home* (2012) deals with the struggles of Frank Money, an African American war veteran. Delineating the typical masculine experiences like the horrors associated with war and its psychological consequences, *Home* offers a space to look into the varied aspects of male friendship and the responsibilities of Frank as a brother. Returning to the Americas of 1950s, Morrison exposes the bigotry and the racist treatment an African American had to experience in his journey to Georgia to save his sister. What Frank had to experience in the form of cultural and racial trauma is amply put forth through the first person and third person narrative in *Home*.

*God Help the Child* (2015), Morrison's last novel, is perhaps a re-journey of the experiences of an African American girl who is traumatised due to her blackness, with the agents of victimisation being her own family. Echoing the notion of childhood trauma as depicted in *The Bluest Eye*, Morrison paints Bride as the traumatized child whose childhood experiences voice the injustice which the Black community cannot surpass and emerge positively.

## Part II

THE ARRAY of intellectual and scholarly works on the corpus of Morrison's works clearly points out the heterogeneous form of criticism which Morrison's works had received all across the world. Readings touching on diverse critical perspectives and theoretical approaches in Morrison's works have contributed a lot in creating and enhancing a distinct consciousness pertaining to the African American identity. While the world in Morrison's works clearly calls for a serious discussion on the cultural, political and social dimensions centering on the debated lives of the African Americans in the United States, Morrison's narrative space invites even more thought provoking and productive dialogue so as to make the world a better place to live in. This aim forms the foci of this edited volume where the essays would attempt to provide some valuable insights and suggestions grounding on the works of Morrison.

European colonists saw America either as a garden, a place of great abundance, as was the case of Captain Arthur Barlowe, or as a wilderness, as was the case of William Bradford. In Morrison's *A Mercy*, even though one can see the vision of

America as a garden, in the way, for example, that the indigenous people approached and took sustenance from the land, it is the colonizing myth of America as a dark and trying wilderness that had to be conquered, subdued, and possessed to create the garden of abundance that Morrison explores in greater detail, since, ultimately, it is the myth that became the driving force in the making of America. Dokubo Melford Goodhead in his chapter 'The Wilderness as a Character in Toni Morrison's A Mercy' attempts to explore how Morrison presents the wilderness as an active character, which always provides choices to the other characters in the novel, choices that either help to draw out their common humanity from them and lead them to a place of co-existence and cooperation with one another or one of separation and individualism after their limited vision of community.

Moloi's chapter "Eurocentrism and African Cultural Disintegration: An Exploration of Ideological Reflections from Maulana Karenga's Idea of Kawaida and Toni Morrison's Ideas in *The Bluest Eye*" provides an Afrocentric conceptual intervention to reflect on the impact of Eurocentrism on African cultural crisis through the reconstruction of African identities and the production of the Black inferiority complex syndrome. The chapter draws from the works of two renowned African American scholars and activists, namely, Maulana Karenga's idea of *Kawaida* and Toni Morrison's reflections on identity, race and gender as captured in her novel *The Bluest Eye*, with the objective to address the cultural crisis among African people cross-continentally. This chapter emphasizes the significance of re-grounding African people within their own cultural ethos as a base from which to reconstruct their identities to overcome Eurocentric oppressive and divisive culture.

Toni Morrison's novels have continued to attract the attention of critics and scholars both because of their political content and literary qualities. Reading her fictional writings within the context of the Black Lives Matter protests, Abdelkader Ben Rhit's chapter "Post What ? The Disarticulation of Post-Racial Discourse in Toni Morrison's novels" examines the quest for freedom that is still an ongoing phenomenon for the African American community in the purportedly 'post-racial' America. The idea of freedom, which is central in Morrison novels, has been powerfully affected by slavery, racism, sexism, injustice and inequality in the American society. Almost all Morrison's novels have been remarkable for their divergent routes of the quest for freedom. Like the Black Lives Matter protests, Morrison's novels have attempted to shake the White people's collective memories out of dis-remembrance of coloured lives and to demand accountability from abusers. This chapter analyses *The Bluest Eye, Sula, Song of Solomon, Tar Baby, and Beloved* from the Black feminist perspective. It focuses on what Morrison calls the 'disremembered and unaccounted for'—it mainly examines the African American female protagonists' journey of struggle for survival, their protest against the various forms of oppression they have been subject to by both White and African American people, and finally their liberation and assertion of their identities. This chapter investigates how the female protagonists' quest for freedom and for a sense of self emerges from agonising experiences of exploitation, marginalisation and denial, how their self-knowledge is reached through the long traumatic process of mourning and of awakening to another self. It argues that suffering for the African American women is empowering rather than paralysing. Morrison herself states, 'what is heroic that's the way I know why such people survive' and it's this 'way' and this 'why' which this chapter explores at length.

Bhawana Pokharel's chapter "Female Body in Toni Morrison's Novels: A Case of *Home* and *Beloved*" discusses how Morrison's women characters undergo the derogation and fragmentation of their bodies. It explores how such physically and psychologically disintegrated females in the novels feel disconnected from themselves as well as from the community. The novels depict that women are forcefully splintered from their 'selves' by patriarchy and slavery. Patriarchy always tends to have control over women's bodies as well as their minds. Likewise, racism relegates women to the level of sexual objects. The physical and sexual assault inflicted by patriarchy and racism casts a bodily and psychological fragmentation upon women. The chapter primarily interrogates into the experiences of Cee and Sethe along with other women characters and demonstrates how the violated women eventually, with hope, seek to abridge the rift through protest and revenge allowing solidarity to harvest healing.

Fairy tales often depend upon the transformation of the characters from weak to strong, from vulnerable to victorious, from invisible to visible. This seems to be a part of Toni Morrison's message in her outstanding nonfiction work *Playing in the Dark*, in which she explores the structure of society built on whiteness as the comparative norm, and how that norm is reflected in the national literature. People of color became invisible to the Whites—as explored in Ralph Ellison's *Invisible Man*—because Whites are blinded by their own worldview, caught in a cultural mindset that is not easy to escape. It takes a shift from willful ignorance to conscious examination of the self and the other. In the chapter "*Playing in the Dark* and the American Fairy Tale", Tamara Miles examines *Playing in the Dark* as a lens that can help people live out the more authentic human experience that rises above play-acting and fairy tales.

Motherhood is a central and recurring theme in Morrison's novels and she also invests in this subject frequently in her essays, lectures and interviews. She revises and scrutinizes motherhood, a traditional space of security, to contextualize her narratives against the oppressive socio-cultural contexts against which the African Americans had to survive in America for centurie. From her first novel *The Bluest Eye* to her last, *God Help the Child* Morrison has delved deep into the psychological scar and trauma generated by the troubled mother-child relationship. In her ninth novel *A Mercy*, Morrison again engages with the vulnerability of mother-daughter relationship to underscore the humanity of African American mothers forced to operate within inhuman pressure exercised by slavery. Set in colonial America *A Mercy* is an exploration of the broken mother-daughter relationship which results in psychic rupture and imparity of communication. Saikat's chapter "Of Unspeaking Mothers and Unforgiving Daughters: Reading the Trauma of Broken Mother-Child Relation in *A Mercy*" attempts to examine how in her novels in general and *A Mercy* in particular, Morrison builds upon and re-inscribes on the difficult experiences of African American women as mothers to form a different perspective of motherhood. Additionally, the chapter also attempts to explore how Morrison constructs a distinctive view of African American motherhood in her novel which demands to be approached and understood as radically different from the image of motherhood ingrained in and endorsed by the dominant White American culture.

*The Bluest Eye*, since its publication in 1970, has been subjected to readings of diverse perspectives, often engaging the text as a platform to trace elements of violence, suffering, rejection, trauma and racist consciousness from the vantage point of feminism, psychoanalysis and trauma theories. Morrison's efforts to tap into the cruelty of racial configuration alongside the journey of an innocent African American girl child to insanity, is heart wrenching, which forms the foci of Raju's chapter "Desire, Disappointment and Derangement: Pecola's Progression from Innocence to Insanity in Toni Morrison's *The Bluest Eye*".

To deal with (in)visibility in an American context, which is racially segregated, one has to go beyond its dictionary definition because people of colour experience invisibility due to the historical, social, cultural and economic conditions marking their existence. The invisibility of coloured races in America is not due to their skin colour as much as it is due to the institution that is used to define their existence in America i.e., slavery. Morrison engages not only through her fiction writing but also through her critical attempts in understanding the invisibility of her fellow countrymen, three centuries after the abolishment of slavery. She believes that it is time for readers, critics and artists to be cured from 'willful critical blindness' (18)—such blindness is the consequence of institutions 'like slavery' (33). The direct impact of her critical writing *Playing in the Dark* can be traced in *Beloved*. With her emphasis on American Africanism, the text stages Morrison's debate about the legacy of slavery that resulted in a haunted presence of the Black self. The given paper offers a re-reading of the haunting presence of slavery that denied the Black self a visible presence. In the light of the critical findings of *Playing in the Dark,* Kortas' chapter aims to trigger a new reading of *Beloved.*

Morrison's contributions to the literary field form the crux of the discussion of Nitesh Narolia's chapter which attempts to cover Morrison's contribution to African American literature and society by exploring her as a feminist, a post-colonial critic and a womanist. It also aims to explore the historical representation in her works while analyzing the narrative and language of her works.

Sneha Sawai's chapter "Reclaiming Oneself: Subaltern Perspectives in Toni Morrison's *Beloved*" discusses the idea of the subaltern in *Beloved.* It delves into the complexity of being an African American woman in a male dominated racist society. It also looks at how through the use of the narrative technique of stream-of-consciousness an alternate historiography that challenges the Eurocentric discourse is constructed.

Morrison was deeply engaged with the issues of race, gender, love, sexuality and oppression. Parui's chapter "Sexual Power Politics: A Critique of Toni Morrison's *Sula*" primarily focuses on the relationship between gender and sexual politics. She uses divergent sexualities to show the impact of the social milieu on the character's mind, body, feelings, emotions and deeds. Sexual politics suggest a vivid association of the gender roles in society with which the novel is set. It aims to show the ruin of the protagonist and a cordial friendship between two girls turning to womanhood with the conflict of an unequal balance between the genders in the society and non-functional relations and ruined individuals. This novel presents different sexual codes which splits the community and ruptures relationships by society's traditional gender codes. Ailing sexuality is a symbolic manifestation of the ailing community and society as well. This chapter will unearth the question of social identity out of sexual politics in relation to *Sula*.

One of the most remarkable features of Morrison's *Sula* is the total absence of Whites. The evil is internal. The suffering is among themselves and the only blame they can find is in sleeping with the Whites. When they have to term Sula as evil, they assume that she slept with the Whites in the cities. This is psychological segregation that an African American writer reveals to the world. Morrison attacks the critics of African American writers with the following words in the 2004 Foreword of the Vintage Classics, 'Whether they were wholly uninterested in politics of any sort, or whether they were politically inclined, aware, or aggressive, the fact of their race or the race of their characters doomed them to a 'political-only' analysis of their worth.' (page XI) Thus, Anuradha Bhattacharya's chapter "Magical Realism in Toni Morrison's *Sula*" attempts to locate the artistry in Morrison.

Both Morrison and Alice Walker, the most significant women writers in the canon of African American literature depict suffering, humiliation, exploitation and marginalization of the Black people in general and African American women in particular. During the 17$^{th}$ century, the slave trade in America brought people from several African nations to America as labours, where they remained as slaves for centuries. Racial discrimination in White racist America made their lives vulnerable. They found their existence meaningless and faced trauma of alienation in the alien land. The condition of women was more pathetic who faced triple jeopardy of race, gender and class. The problem of existence faced by the Black people is well presented in the works of Toni Morrison and Alice Walker. Vijay Songire's chapter "Existentialism in Toni Morrison's *The Bluest Eye* and Alice Walker's *Meridian*" investigates the issues of existentialism. The chapter attempts to show how both the writers are similar in their portrayal of existentialism in their respective novels. They have shown existential predicament of the characters in their novels.

There is no doubt that Afro-American women novelists have contributed in the painting of the New World's phantasmagoria. Such authors, as Margaret Mitchell, Ellen Glasgow, and Carson MacCullers, have put into light many feminist values that used to be deserted under the shadow of a highly patriarchal society. Morrison's *Beloved* is one of the pioneering works in this field. Set in rural Ohio, at the time of the American Civil War, Morrison puts forward an unprecedented portrait of a shattered identity, feminine resistance, as well as humiliating conditions of racism. Yet, the novel also adapts the developing status of African American women in the American society which becomes the focal point of discussion in Aya Somrani's chapter "Toni Morrison's Role in Feminine Social Revolution expressed in *Beloved*". Perceived from this perspective, Afro-American women's novels are not ready recipes. They are rather born out of long endured agony and social controversy, leading them to the final stage of self-establishment.

Toni Morrison occupies a distinctive place in the realm of contemporary African American fiction. Morrison's major interest lies in doing justice to female points of view, concerns, and values in all her works. One of the several concerns of Morrison is to present feminine subject matters such as the world of domesticity, of gestation, giving birth and nurturing, of mother-daughter, woman-woman, and man-woman relations. Another significant concern of Morrison is to show a feminine mode of experience, or 'subjectivity', in thinking, feeling, valuing, and perceiving oneself and the outer world. Morrison, beginning with organizing psychological traumas, has travelled to reveal her female protagonist's quest for self-identity. There is reconciliation, compromise, helpless resignation but no solace at the end of her novels. Morrison is excellent in depicting the inner furies of women and their rising tone for emancipation and empowerment. She makes known to us the unconscious motifs of female psyche. Her novels are powerful descriptions of feminine sensibility. Poonam Mor's chapter "Scapegoat for the Humiliation and Pain as depicted in Toni Morrison's *The Bluest Eye*" unravels the consequences of racism coupled with the imposition of the White beauty standards upon an innocent young African American girl, Pecola.

Thus, through the different perspectives and interpretations of Toni Morrison's works, this anthology serves as a witness to her legacy and her literary brilliance.

## Works Cited

Kubitschek, Missy Dehn. *Toni Morrison: A Critical Companion.* Greenwood Press, 1998.

Mbalia, Dorothea Drummond. "*Tar Baby*: A Reflection of Morrison's Developed Class Consciousness." *Toni Morrison*, edited by Linden Peach, Macmillan Press Ltd, 1998.

McKay, Nellie. "An Interview with Toni Morrison." *Conversations with Toni Morrison*, edited by Danille Taylor- Guthrie, U of Mississippi P, 1994, pp. 138-155.

Samuels, Wilfred D., and Clenora Hudson-Weems, editors. *Toni Morrison*. Twayne Publishers, 1990.

Rodrigues, Eusebio L. "Experiencing Jazz." *Toni Morrison*, edited by Linden Peach, Macmillan Press Ltd, 1998.

Roynon, Tessa. *The Cambridge Introduction to Toni Morrison*. Cambridge UP, 2013.

Zamalin, Alex. "Beloved Citizens: Toni Morrison's Beloved, Racial Inequality, and American Public Policy." Women's Studies Quarterly, vol. 42, no. 1/2, 2014, pp. 205-211, *JSTOR*, www.jstor.org/stable/24364924.

SECTION ONE

# APARTHEID, REFLECTIONS AND DISINTEGRATION

CHAPTER 1

# The Wilderness as a Character in *A Mercy*

Dokubo Melford Goodhead

## Introduction

EUROPEAN COLONISTS saw America either as a garden, a place of great abundance, as was the case of Captain Arthur Barlowe, or as wilderness, as was the case of William Bradford. In Morrison's *A Mercy (2009)*, even though one can see the vision of America as a garden, for example, in how the land's indigenous people approached and took sustenance from the land, it is the colonizing myth of America as a dark and trying wilderness that had to be conquered, subdued, and possessed to create the garden of abundance that Morrison explores in greater detail, since, ultimately, it is the myth that became the driving force in the making of America. In Morrison's exploration of the myth and the driving force that it gave to the colonists, she presents the wilderness as an active character, which is always presenting choices to the other characters in the novel—choices that either help to draw out their common humanity from them and lead them to a place of co-existence and cooperation with one another, or one of separation and individualism after their limited vision of community.

These two overarching visions—America as garden and America as wilderness—are unambiguously present in two of the most important historical documents that captured the encounters between the colonial visitors and the indigenous communities whose land would later be seized by the former. The act of colonizing the lands of the indigenous communities is further historicized in colonial documents as a case of the lands being empty or without inhabitants or as a case of those who inhabited them being of no consequence. In 1584, Captain Arthur Barlowe, who was financed by Sir Walter Raleigh—an explorer and courtier in the court of Queen Elizabeth I—made an exploratory voyage to America to look into the possibility of planting a colony on the sub-continent. Barlowe made landfall at Roanoke Island and wrote about his experience in *Captain Arthur Barlowe's Narrative of the First Voyage to the Coast of America* (2013). A number of things stand out in Barlowe's narrative—the abundant natural riches of the land; the friendly reception that Barlowe, his co-captain on the voyage Philip Amadas, and their crew received from the Native Algonquin; the lopsidedness in the value of the goods that the visitors exchanged with the Algonquin; and the unselfconscious claiming of the land by the visitors for Queen Elizabeth I and England. The land was everything that Barlowe had come to find. A shoal off the island made him and his crew feel as if they were 'in the midst of a delicate garden abounding with all kinds of odoriferous flowers…' (32). The island's natural resources were profuse (33). However, although the Algonquins were friendly to Barlowe and his men, it did not deter the latter from making an unfair exchange of goods with them in which they exchanged trifles for precious commodities. Barlowe writes, 'We exchanged our tinne dish for twentie skins woorth twentie Crownes, or twentie Nobles and a copper kettle for fifty skins woorth fifty Crownes,' (34) establishing a tradition of lopsided commercial exchanges between Europeans and the indigenous tribes. Barlowe's account of the new Eden and his crew and his tremendous good fortune would pave the way for the planting of Jamestown, the first successful English colony in America, in 1607, and the arrival of William Bradford and his fellow pilgrims in the Mayflower at New Plymouth, New England in 1620. The pilgrims saw the new land through different eyes from those of Barlowe's. They saw a wilderness, not a garden. Bradford gives us his impression, 'Besides, what could they see but a hideous and desolate wilderness, fall [sic] of wild beasts and wild men—and what multitudes there might be of them they knew not' (62). A scouting team from the party found a place where some of the local Wampanoag had kept their harvest of corn and beans. It was a fortuitous find for the pilgrims, for as Bradford puts it, 'And here is to be noted a special providence of God, and a great mercy to this poor people, that here they got seed to plant them corn the next year, or else they might have starved...' (66). The pilgrims would in all likelihood have suffered the fate of the first settlers of the Jamestown colony without the propitious find of the beans and corn in the granary of the Wampanoag, because they landed during a harsh winter. However, this did not provoke an epiphany in Bradford and the pilgrims, that the Wampanoag were indeed like them, not savages. Histories like these influenced Morrison in *A Mercy.* As Mark Sandy has noted in his reading of the novel, 'Within the American tradition, the site of the pastoral is infrequently aligned with the idealizing imagination and epiphany and more often with the realities of aggressive colonial ownership of the land and its people' (36). Like Barlowe, before them, they immediately made a claim to the land, one that they could not make of the city of Leiden, in the Netherlands, where they had stayed ten years, after fleeing religious persecution in England.

Bradford was fairly widely read for the age in which he lived. According to S.E. Morison, the editor of the 1952 edition of the *Of Plymouth Plantation: 1620-1647*, 'Largely through his own efforts he learned Dutch and a certain amount of Latin and Hebrew, and acquired a wide knowledge of general literature and a fair-sized library...' (xxiii). Notably, one of the people that Bradford had read was the stoic philosopher, Seneca, whom he makes almost immediate mention of in his account of the settlement of the Plymouth colony. As we know, the stoic philosophers, both of ancient Greece and Rome, were the source of cosmopolitan thought, the idea of looking at the other—the stranger—as kin in Western philosophy. Bradford had read stoic philosophy but did not apply its teachings to the Wampanoag. This is especially telling because the pilgrims fled religious persecution in England to Leiden and could only stay there by appealing to the good graces of their Dutch hosts. In contrast, they imposed themselves on the Wampanoag, seizing control of the land of the Wampanoag, as if it was theirs by right. It should be said though that the pilgrims were doing nothing different from what had been done through the ages. The militarily stronger took advantage of the militarily weaker. The pilgrims had muskets. The Wampanoag had bows and arrows. The fighting technology of the pilgrims, as was the case of the settlers of the Jamestown colony, was superior to that of the indigenous tribes and nations whose lands they took by force. At the same time, the pilgrims, like every other colonizer in history, could justify their forceful seizure of Wampanoag land by *othering* them as 'savage barbarians' (62), even though the Wampanoag had held the land for thousands of years before the pilgrims and other colonizers set foot on the land and were the notable source of the farm produce that saved the pilgrims from almost certain death through starvation, a fate that befell many of the first settlers of the Jamestown colony. Here, it is worth asking like Morrison does in *Playing in the Dark* (1992), 'Why is it [the land] seen as raw and savage? Because it is peopled by a non-white indigenous population?' (45).

The fact is that Bradford's likely familiarity with the cosmopolitan philosophy of the stoics and its counterpart in Christian theology, that of loving one's neighbor as oneself and doing unto others what one would want others to do to one, did not prevent him and his fellow pilgrims from acting from a position of pure self-interest. However, this does not mean that others like him, who were familiar with cosmopolitan philosophy, did not ponder the great disparity between theory and practice in the conduct of their fellow Europeans in their voyages around the world that ultimately shaped the world into one of colonizers and colonized. By the eighteenth century, enough data had accumulated from these voyages for Immanuel Kant to sift them through the lens of cosmopolitan philosophy. The right of the European visitor, or stranger, to the lands he was colonizing, Kant writes, 'does not extend further than the conditions of the *possibility of entering into social intercourse* with the inhabitants of the country' (102). The European visitor could not impose himself on his host (101). He goes on to talk of the injustice of the Europeans, who:

> in their first contact with foreign lands and peoples fills us even with horror, the mere *visiting* of such peoples being regarded by them as equivalent to a *conquest.* America, the Negro Lands, the Spice Islands, the Cape of Good Hope, etc., on being discovered, were treated as countries that belonged to nobody; for the Aboriginal inhabitants were reckoned as nothing. In the East Indies, under the pretext of intending merely to plant commercial settlements, the Europeans introduced foreign troops, and with them oppression of the Natives, instigation of the different States to widespread wars, famine, sedition, perfidy, and all the litany of evils that can oppress the human race (102).

Kant goes on to observe that it is no wonder that both China and Japan restricted the visit of Europeans, with Japan taking the very stringent measure of permitting only the Dutch into the country and once they entered the country excluding them 'from social intercourse with the Natives' (103).

*A Mercy* is Morrison's cosmopolitan philosophical meditation on the making of America, in the seventeenth century, after nearly a century of European settlement and not long after the Nathaniel Bacon insurrection of 1675-1676 in Jamestown made the Virginia colonists to unleash a set of laws that would ultimately make Black servitude a permanent status. The novel, which begins in the year 1682, is what Leo Marx would call a complex pastoral, in which the writer calls into question and writes with irony about 'the illusion of peace and harmony in a green pasture' (25). The novel's complexity as a pastoral derives from the fact that it is an eco-literary work in which the natural environment, in this instance the wilderness, is not merely presented as the background against which the characters live their lives or create history but is important in itself and whose integrity must be respected by the novel's human characters. The wilderness, therefore, emerges as a major character in the novel, nudging the other characters towards a cosmopolitan relationship with each other in order to withstand the challenges of living on the frontier. Individualism in the face of its challenges is self-defeating and even calamitous. Morrison realizes this narrative through various sets of relationships that revolve around the novel's protagonist, Jacob Vaark, his relationship with those he has brought into his household as well as his and their relationship with other characters in the novel at a time when race as we know it today had not yet crystalized in the consciousness of Americans.

## Jacob Vaark and Madelina (Lina): Orphans that Found Each Other and Tried to Create a Garden in the Wilderness

In *Playing in the Dark: Whiteness and the Literary Imagination*, Morrison talks at length about William Dunbar, a young Scottish immigrant to colonial America. Dunbar was no ordinary Scot. He was a product of the Scottish Enlightenment and had engaged in correspondence on, amongst other things, the beatitudes of Jonathan Swift, enjoining that mankind 'love one another' (41). However, as Morrison notes quite significantly, in July 1776, what Dunbar recorded in his diary was not the nation's historic independence, but a conspiracy for freedom by those that he had enslaved on his plantation

(41). Dunbar is shocked that the enslaved had plotted to free themselves, even though he was right in the midst of the ferment of revolutionary sentiment arising from the American Revolution, a child of the Enlightenment. He orders that each of the conspirators be given 2500 lashes (45). The difficulties of frontier life had not turned Dunbar into a philosopher in the wilderness practicing what he had learnt from Swift's beatitudes or the Enlightenment rhetoric of liberty that Thomas Jefferson captures in the most famous lines of *The Declaration of Independence*, "We hold these truths to be self-evident, that all men are created equal, that they are endowed by their Creator with certain unalienable Rights, that among these are Life, Liberty and the pursuit of Happiness."[1] Like Bradford, who was knowledgeable in cosmopolitan philosophy, a driving principle of the Enlightenment, Dunbar had succumbed to pure self-interest. About sixteen years after Morrison engaged in her public reflection on William Dunbar, she would create a character in *A Mercy* who would start out with Dunbar's cosmopolitan sentiments, not from a life of learning, but from a life of experiencing what it means to be an orphan, who is looked down upon in society. This character is Jacob Vaark.

Vaark's life as an orphan has turned him into a cosmopolitan, one who sees all of humanity as kith and kin and deserving of good faith and kindness. We see this not only in the kindness and consideration that he shows towards the women in his

---

1 Jefferson, Thomas. "Declaration of Independence." *National Archives*, The U.S. National Archives and Records Administration, 4 July 1776, www.archives.gov/founding-docs/declaration-transcript.

household but in the way that he interacts with the blacksmith.

> Sir behaved as though the blacksmith was his brother. Lina had seen them bending their heads over lines drawn in dirt. Another time she saw Sir slice a green apple, his left boot raised on a rock, his mouth working along with his hands; the smithy nodding, looking intently at his employer. Then Sir, as nonchalantly as you please, tipped a slice of apple on his knife and offered it to the blacksmith who, just as nonchalantly, took it and put in his mouth (71).

As an adult, Vaark still remembers very clearly the life that he had lived on the streets of London and how he had spent a "stint in a poorhouse before the luck of being taken on as a runner for a law firm" (38). He can see his travails as an orphan in the travails of others, even animals. This, in part, is what informs his purchase of Lina to help him with work on the farm. He had inherited from an uncle 'one hundred and twenty [acres] of woodland that was located some seven miles from a hamlet founded by Separatists' (38), suddenly making him a man who owns property. But he soon finds out that he is a poor farmer and that to succeed in frontier life he needs a partner to do the work with him, which is to create a garden out of the wilderness. It is into this void that Lina steps. Like him, she is an orphan. However, more importantly, Morrison uses Lina's story to demonstrate the devastation that diseases like smallpox, that Europeans brought with them to America, had on the Native tribes and nations. Except her and two little boys, Lina's entire village is wiped out by the disease. 'Infants fell silent first, and even as their mothers heaped earth over their bones, they too were pouring sweat and limp as maize hair. At first, they fought off the crows, she and two young boys, but they were no match for the birds or the smell…' (54). This is one of the numerous instances in the novel where it reveals itself as a complex pastoral text. As Geneva Cobb Moore has noted, 'Morrison is neither playful nor romantic in her quest to teach the hellish history of the marginalized Other in mainstream American history…' (35). Beyond their totally devastated village, the children face the wilderness and a lake. Then, out of the wilderness appear 'men in blue uniforms', who rescue them (54). Cooperation and cosmopolitan coexistence are a persistent theme that runs through the novel. The men in blue uniforms turn Lina over to a Presbyterian family, who after adjudging her of being incapable of full conversation to their doctrines, puts her up for sale after one of their fellow Europeans in the town physically abuses her with a whip, leaving her with a swollen eye and 'lash cuts on her face, arms, and legs...' (61). Thus, she is ready to begin a new life when she meets Vaark. Like him, she is an orphan, who has seen much suffering. However, he is a poor farmer, so, though, quite younger than him, she has a lot to teach him about the art of survival in the wilderness and creating a garden, a farm, out of it.

With Vaark, Morrison strips away the romanticism surrounding frontier life in the sentimental pastoral, exposing as false the myth of the self-made frontiersman who raises a homestead or becomes a prosperous farmer all by himself. Mara Willard has said that in the novel, Morrison 'illuminates[s] the impoverished background of the early Europeans…' (4). Frontier life is difficult. Behind the successful homesteader or farmer are others, either family members or the enslaved. Coming from city life, Vaark is ill-equipped to do the work of turning the wilderness into a garden. Lina often catches him 'staring at the sky as if in wondering despair at the land's refusal to obey his will' (57). But Vaark's frustrations with the bewildering wilderness does not turn him into a William Dunbar. Susan Strehle has argued that 'In many ways, Vaark reflects the best traits and intentions of the American pioneer…' (113). In his relationship with Lina, Morrison paints an alternative vision, a different narrative to the one that gave birth to the country.

The vicissitudes of the wilderness do not create a master-slave relationship between him and Lina, even though Lina is technically his slave. Rather, he embraces a partnership with her, where each of them brings to the partnership a skill that the other does not have. Having grown up in the midst of Nature, Lina possesses a stock of knowledge about the wilderness and seems to intuitively grasp the challenges that the wilderness is always throwing at them and how to respond to the challenges, while, as a former city boy, Vaark is good at 'building things' (58). They work together to create a garden out of the wilderness: 'Together they minded the fowl and starter stock; planted corn and vegetables. But it was she who taught him how to dry the fish they caught; to anticipate spawning and how to protect a crop from night creatures' (57).

Theirs is an exchange that is radically different from the exchange that took place between Captain Barlowe, his crew and the Algonquins and between Bradford, his fellow pilgrims and the Wampanoags. While the latter two situations were non-cosmopolitan relationships, whose goal was colonization and domination of the Natives, Morrison gives an alternative vision of these early encounters between Europeans and Natives, in her representation of the relationship between Vaark and Lina, that points to an America that would have been more in line with the lofty declarations of *The Declaration of Independence.* Vaark has something to teach Lina and Lina has something to teach Vaark. It is the mutual acknowledgement of each other's strengths and weaknesses and willingness to take on the challenges of creating a farm out of the wilderness together, where they would both be happy, that enables them to create a successful farm: their garden in the wilderness. His story, though similar to that of the pilgrims, who preceded him to America by about three-quarters of a century, takes a turn from their own. Like him, they were outcasts from English society. Like him, they, too, left England for the Netherlands, from where they made the journey to America. However, unlike them, he gives recognition to the other—as a human being of equal standing—not a savage.

Though Morrison creates an archetypal Adam and Eve couple in Vaark and Lina, who have to eat from the sweat of their toil, in their creation of a garden in the wilderness, she does not stay with that narrative. I read Morrison's turn away from that narrative as one of awareness on her part that it will present an allegorical reading that would seem to confirm exactly what she is writing against: the European colonizer taking possession of a feminine land represented by Lina. Justine Tally has said with very good reason that she reads the novel as an allegory (66). The work can indeed be read as an allegory. However, it seems to me that in not pairing Vaark and Lina as man and wife, even though she represents Vaark as a cosmopolitan, who truly regards all men and women as kith and kin, she avoids the kind of allegorical reading that would represent Lina as the feminine land, which the European, Vaark, comes to husband, hence the entrance of Rebekka, whose presence in the novel gives Morrison a wider scope to engage this period of American history. The entrance of Rebekka is also a complication of history—the formation of a sisterhood between the indigenous woman and the European woman.

## Lina and Rebekka: From Passive-Aggressive Confrontation to Sisterhood

In 1782, the congress of the United States passed an act to include what had been the unofficial motto of the young nation, the phrase *E Pluribus Unum*, 'Out of many one,' on the seal of the nation. Morrison's setting of *A Mercy* to begin exactly a century before this event, when the concept of race had not yet taken root, is quite telling. She explores an important aspect of the 'Out of many one' motto in the Vaark household, sisterhood between the European woman and the indigenous woman. The relationship does not start well. 'When the European wife stepped down from the cart, hostility between them was instant' (61). The two women quickly discover though that the wilderness is a difficult place and that for them to overcome the myriad challenges that it daily presents to them, they have to work together (62). This becomes even more important after Vaark and Rebekka fall out with their closest neighbours, Anabaptist separatists. The two women form a sisterhood, building the homestead in ways that give the lie to myths and narratives of masculine heroism about homesteading on the frontier. The labour of the women in the domestic sphere is shown as crucial to the success of the homestead, community formation, and ultimately the nation itself.

The homestead on the frontier cannot succeed without the domestic labour of its women, especially in one where labour is not that which enslaved persons must do, with a Dunbar or a D'Ortega wielding the whip over them. In such egalitarian environment, petty quarrels quickly begin to look foolish as the challenges of living in the wilderness stare down at one and all. Consequently, '[T]he animosity [between the two women], utterly useless in the wild, died in the womb' (62). Morrison writes about everyday chores such as harvesting berries, milking the cows, keeping the foxes away, 'when to handle and spread manure' and what to feed the baby for a healthy bowel function. We rarely find such information in history books, as they mainly record the deeds of men. Yet, as Morrison reminds us, in so far as it is the successful homestead that enables the establishment of the successful community on the frontier and it is the successful community that is at the very heart of nation formation in a new nation, these domestic chores are as important as the deeds of men that find their way into history books.

In this phase of the relationship between Lina and Rebekka, we see the true meaning of *E Pluribus Unum*, a gesture towards cosmopolitanism, as the two women move from antagonists to friends. Estranged from their closest neighbours, the Anabaptists, and with Vaark taking up trade and money lending, they have to rely on each other. Lina becomes the midwife to Rebekka and helps to deliver all her babies. In the context of 'out of many one', Lina, thus, stands in a metaphoric role, as the Native mediator through which the American nation is born. As such, I suggest that the death of Rebekka's children points to the very problematic elision of the Native from the actual formation of the nation. *E Pluribus Unum* was exclusionary to the indigenous peoples of the land, who as possessors of the land upon which the European colonizer was trying to bring forth a new nation, in the famous words of Abraham Lincoln, were from the outset displaced as mediators both metaphorically and physically.

Morrison seems to be suggesting that this exclusion constitutes an elision or death at the very core of the nation that would haunt it for a very long time. As Kant has reminded us, the rights of the visitor to a foreign land does not extend beyond the extension of a simple courtesy of social intercourse with him (102). If the Europeans, who voyaged to the various territories that would eventually form the American nation had come as cosmopolitan visitors and not as colonizers, they would have gone through the aborigines of the land as mediators to their settlement of those territories in a similar manner to the settlement at Leiden by Bradford and his fellow pilgrims.

Under these conditions, a truly cosmopolitan society would have emerged in the land that would have been more in keeping with the *E Pluribus Unum* motto of the young nation when it emerged from the land. As it is, the aboriginals were violently displaced from this role, leaving as Morrison dramatizes in the novel, not only a haunting death at the heart of the formation of the emerging nation but also the emergence of *E Pluribus Unum,* a banner that covered only the colonizing Europeans.

## The Wilderness, Separatism, and Individualism

In *Playing in the Dark*, Morrison spends some time to ponder American individualism as well as subject it to a scathing critique. She writes:

> Autonomy is freedom and translates into the much championed and revered 'individualism'; newness translates into 'innocence'; distinctiveness becomes difference and the erection of strategies for maintaining it; authority and absolute power become a romantic, conquering 'heroism,' virility, and the problematics of wielding absolute power over the lives of others. All the rest are made possible by this last, it would seem—absolute power called forth and played against and within a natural and mental Landscape conceived of as a 'raw, half-savage world. (44-45)

The American frontier is the theatre where all of this play out. As we have seen, Vaark is unlike William Dunbar. He does not play out his 'heroism,' 'virility' and 'absolute power' over those under him—Lina, Florens, and Sorrow—and certainly not Rebekka, his wife. 'Morrison declared [that] she sought to make goodness visible, audible, and dignified in her writings' (Willard 478), something she does with Vaark. However, in an interview on the novel, she also noted, 'I wanted this group [the Vaark homestead] to be sort of the earliest version of American individualism, American self-sufficiency, and I think I wanted to show that you really do need a community.'[2] Vaark, however,

2 "Toni Morrison Discusses 'A Mercy.'" www.youtube.com, www.youtube.com/watch?v=7IZvMhQ2LIU. Accessed 1 Mar. 2023.

has decided to isolate himself from the Anabaptists, his nearest neighbours. He 'learned that they had bolted from their brethren over the question of the chosen versus the universal nature of salvation. His neighbours favoured the first and situated themselves inland beyond fur posts and wars' (39). He considers the belief of the splinter sect of Anabaptists that they are the chosen ones to the exclusion of everyone else as blasphemy (39). Consequently, when Rebekka falls out with them over their refusal to baptize her infant children, he cuts off ties with them and takes to individualism.

Morrison critiques individualism, seeing it as flawed, especially in the wilderness where she sees the community as essential, if not for survival, for a fuller realization of the self. This we see in Vaark's life during the time he used to socialize with them in the first and second houses that he built. They 'freely helped Sir build the second house, the outhouses, and happily joined him in felling white pine for the post fence...' (66). Through Lina, we know that 'The first house [he] built—dirt floor, green wood—was weaker than the bark-covered one she herself was born in. The second one,' which the Anabaptists helped him build 'was strong. [It had] wooden floors...four rooms, a decent fireplace and windows with good tight shutters' (50).

In Lina's view, the vicissitudes of the wilderness make being within a community critically essential. To separate oneself from the community is to situate oneself as a primal family, one that comes before all others, one that exists in the absence of others. Since Vaark and Rebekka do not actually occupy that locus, Lina believes that it is pride that makes them act as if they do.

> Their drift away from others produced a selfish privacy and they had lost the refuge and the consolation of a clan. Baptists, Presbyterians, tribe, army, family, some encircling outside thing was needed. Pride, she thought. Pride alone made them think that they needed only themselves, could shape life that way, like Adam and Eve, like gods from nowhere beholden to nothing except their own creations.' (68-69)

Under these circumstances, when catastrophe strikes, there is no one to turn to. Through Lina, Morrison makes her strongest critique of American individualism and exposes the myth of the self-sufficient frontiersman who does it all by himself. The lone frontiersman or even the lone homestead that stands like a hermit in the wilderness. It is the community, Morrison wants us to believe, that helps the individual in the wilderness to not only adequately take on the challenges of the wilderness but to do so in a way that gives fulness to life in a such a demanding environment.

## The Wilderness and the City

The conceit that the city spells corruption while the garden spells harmonious co-existence with nature has been around since the time of Theocritus and the *Eclogues*. Vaark has been able to carve out his garden in the middle of the wilderness through forging, as we have seen, first a bond with Lina and, then his wife, Rebekka, Sorrow and Florens. He has lost three children in their infancy and a five-year old to the kick of a horse and Rebekka is no longer as 'cheerful as a bluebird' (23) but despite the hardships of the wilderness and the loss of his children, a sense of contentment and peace, arising from what he and the three women have been able to achieve by carving out an oasis in the midst of the wilderness (24) and his hope that as a young, healthy couple, he and Rebekka, would have 'more children and at least one, a boy, would live to thrive' (24), has crept into the household. Being an orphan, who arrived in America with nothing, he has achieved the American Dream. However, he does not take what he has achieved from a position of utter nothing as an orphan—sixty acres of cultivated wilderness and sixty additional acres of uncultivated wilderness, the love of his wife, and a contented household—as enough wealth, so he goes into money lending, which ultimately takes him to the city, the colony of Maryland, to collect a debt from the wealthy slave dealer, Senhor D'Ortega. I call the Maryland colony a city, because it has its own seaport, taverns, and elite like D'Ortega, who has created a nouveau rich merchant class or bourgeoisie. Its seaport must be of some size, for we learn that the wealthy slave dealer and owner had just lost a third of his enslaved cargo to disease, thrown away 'their bodies too close to the bay' and had incurred a fine of 'five thousand pounds of tobacco' (18). Broke, Senhor D'Ortega tries to compel Vaark into taking payment in enslaved bodies (25). Viscerally opposed to slavery, from his experience as an orphan, he winces. 'Flesh was not his commodity' (25). It is the same experience as an orphan that persuades him to take Florens, a young girl, whose mother is desperate to protect her from being raped, a misfortune she had suffered. 'Please, Senhor,' the mother, who is with an infant boy, whom she would have left behind if he had followed through with his wish to take her just to spite Senhor D'Ortega, pleads with him. 'Not me. Take my daughter' (30). He shows an act of mercy to the mother by taking the daughter and walks away knowing that he has not corrupted his principle—opposition to slavery.

> Vaark sneered at wealth dependent on a captured workforce that required more force to maintain. Thin as they were, the dregs of his kind of Protestantism recoiled at whips, chains and armed overseers. He was determined to prove that his own industry could amass the fortune, the station, D'Ortega claimed without trading his conscience for coin. (32)

However, a seed of corruption, in the form of his covetous admiration of Senhor D'Ortega's imposing mansion has stolen into his consciousness.

> [I]n spite of himself, [he] envied the house, the gate, the fence.... [M]ighten it be nice to have such a fence to enclose the headstones in his own meadow? And one day, not too far away, to build a house that size on his own property? On that rise in back, with a better prospect of the hills and the valley between them? (32-33)

With the seed of corruption sown in his consciousness, it becomes only a matter of time before his cosmopolitan view of the world is challenged.

The challenge to his principled opposition to slavery comes swiftly. He goes to the tavern to put up his feet for the night and there meets Peter Downes talking about the great wealth to be made from rum, which is made from sugarcane plantations, with very high mortality amongst the enslaved men and women who work on them. The historian, Paul Doolan, tells us, 'In the mid-17th century, British-owned Barbados rapidly developed into a slave society growing sugarcane' (18). In the eighteenth century, he writes, 'The tiny British island of Barbados alone would receive nearly half a million slaves...' (18). We can easily infer from the huge flow of enslaved persons into the small island that the mortality rate amongst the enslaved population must be very high. But the profit to be made from rum was also enormous. 'In a month,' Downes says, 'the time of the journey from mill to Boston, a man can turn fifty pounds into five times as much' (36). Vaark is seduced by the idea and persuades himself to believe that 'there was a profound difference between the intimacy of slave bodies at Jublio and a remote labor force in Barbados' (40). With the enormous wealth from the rum trade, he would be able to build a mansion to rival that of Senhor D'Ortega, 'a grand house of many rooms rising on a hill above the fog' (41).

But Vaark's decision would prove to be catastrophic. He has lived by a principled opposition to slavery, drawn chiefly from a cosmopolitanism forged by his experiences as a destitute orphan and as a homesteader, whose farming practices are informed by what is good for the environment, even when it costs him financially. Speaking through the consciousness of Lina, the narrator says of the eco-friendly farming practices of his and Rebekka's, as owners of the farm,

> They seemed mindful of a distinction between earth and property, fenced their cattle though their neighbors did not, and although legal to do so, they were hesitant to kill foraging swine. They hoped to live by tillage rather than eat up the land with herds, measures that kept their profit low. (64)

He practices eco-cosmopolitanism here, recognizing that the foraging swine, whom he had likely displaced from their foraging grounds, have as much right to the wilderness as him. However, having sacrificed his cosmopolitan principles to accumulate wealth to build his mansion, he also sacrifices his eco-friendly practices.

He started the farm with Lina, working with her to create a garden in the wilderness, and it is appropriately from her that we get an informed, eco-friendly critique of his turn away from those practices. Lina starts by putting things in perspective. The second house, which the Anabaptists helped him to build is sufficient for the needs of the homestead. 'There was no need for a third' (50). Practicing a radical eco-cosmopolitanism, as I have noted, he was mindful of the integrity of the wilderness and the fate of the animals with whom he shared the wilderness. However, to build the third house, he makes a radical turn against the wilderness. In doing so, he moves away from his keen consciousness about the wilderness, one that he shared with Lina, which she retains and deploys to critique him.

> Lina was unimpressed by the festive mood, the jittery satisfaction of everyone involved, and had refused to enter or go near it. That third and presumably final house that Sir insisted on building distorted sunlight and required the death of fifty trees. (50)

From her eco-friendly perspective, he falls ill and dies after the completion of the house because in destroying such a huge number of trees for his vainglorious project, he invited misfortune on himself (51). Echoing her, Anissa Wardi has said that 'Vaark's death following the loss of the trees indicates what may be considered the primary environmental principle, sounded in various ecological and ecocritical treatises: namely that all living organisms are interrelated and interconnected' (31). While there is no medical correlation between death from the smallpox virus and the death of the trees, there is a sense in which, as Wardi shows, the two are ultimately connected, in the sense that compromising the integrity of the environment in the reckless destruction of wilderness ultimately loops back to have devastating consequences for our survival on the planet. This, I think is the larger point that both Morrison and Wardi are making here.

## Conclusion

Morrison's reflection on William Dunbar in *Playing in the Dark* is a window into the character Jacob Vaark in *A Mercy*. University trained and attuned to the sentiments of the Scottish Enlightenment and the teachings of Dean Swift, Dunbar appeared to be the perfect man to create a new society of people, an Arcadia, where the sentiments of the Enlightenment, which are powerfully captured in *The Declaration of Independence*, would be given full play. But Dunbar endured the journey across the Atlantic with one overarching mission—to make himself a wealthy man and to achieve the lordly status that he was unable to achieve in his native Scotland. He goes into the wilderness to raise a farm and there he is put to the test. The wilderness is a place of severe tests and great difficulties. However, the very difficulties that it throws up are also the site where cosmopolitanism can be created, where class and rank can fall away, and where the human spirit can rise to be the best that it can be. The opposite is, of course, also true. The trials of the wilderness, combined with the individualistic pursuit of wealth and lordly status, can turn any man towards his basest instincts. Thus, Dunbar, the student of the Enlightenment, does not see the irony in his anger at the attempt to seek freedom by those that he had enslaved, the very freedom that he, along with the new nation, had just won and was in fact in the midst of a revolutionary war against Great Britain. To achieve the vision of the man he wants to be, to Dunbar, the African becomes the savage other in the same way that the Wampanoag was the savage other to Bradford and the pilgrims.

In contrast to Bradford and Dunbar, Jacob Vaark comes by his cosmopolitanism through his experience as a destitute orphan and the outlook on the world to which this experience has furnished him keeps him on the path of a repeating self-examining cosmopolitanism until he is tempted to aspire to the trappings of old-world-style lordship. When he succumbs, what collapses is not just his cosmopolitanism but also his regard for the integrity of the wilderness as a place where one exercises responsible stewardship of the earth. Against the challenges of the wilderness, he had formed a cosmopolitan partnership with his wife, Rebekka, Lina, the Native, Sorrow, born of a European ship captain and an enslaved African woman, and Florens, the daughter of an enslaved African woman. His homestead, therefore, represents in practice the nation's first official motto: *E Pluribus Unum.* His death is also the death of what the homestead he has built represents, as he is the only person without whom those values cannot survive. Looked at this way, *A Mercy* is indeed an allegory but an allegory in which Morrison grapples with the fundamental questions about the birth and making of America, the divide between its lofty ideas of itself and the practice of those ideas, on the one hand, and the attentive recurring self-examination that is required to narrow the distance between lofty ideas and practice on the other. As such, the novel is indeed a complex pastoral, one in which the wilderness, like the other characters, is an active agent.

## Works Cited

Barlowe, *Arthur. Captain Arthur Barlowe's Narrative of the First Voyage to the Coast of America.* In Daisy Martin, *Exploration and Colonial America (1492-1755).* Salem Press, 2013, pp. 31-40.

Beavers, Herman. *Geography and the Political Imaginary in the Novels of Toni Morrison.* Palgrave Macmillan, 2018.

Bradford, William. *Of Plymouth Plantation: 1620-1647.* Edited by Samuel Eliot Morison. Alfred A Knopf, 1952.

Doolan, Paul. "Beyond Profit." *History Today.* Dec. 2019, vol. 69, no. 12, pp. 16-18.

Jefferson, Thomas. "Declaration of Independence." *National Archives,* The U.S. National Archives and Records Administration, 4 July 1776, www.archives.gov/founding-docs/declaration-transcript.

Kant, Immanuel. *Perpetual Peace.* In *Kant's Principles of Politics,* edited and translated by W. Hastie. T. & T. Clark, 1891.

Marx, Leo. *The Machine in the Garden: Technology and the Pastoral Ideal in America.* Oxford University Press, 1964.

Moore, Geneva Cobb. "A Demonic Parody: Toni Morrison's *A Mercy.*" *The Southern Literary Journal,* vol. XLIV, no. 1, Fall 2011, pp. 1-18

Morrison, S.E. "Introduction." William Bradford, *Of Plymouth Plantation: 1620-1647*. Edited by Samuel Eliot Morrison. Alfred A Knopf, 1952.

Morrison, Toni. *A Mercy*. Vintage International, 2009.

—. Interview. <https://www.youtube.com/watch?v=7IZvMhQ2LIU>

—. *Playing in the Dark: Whiteness and the Literary Imagination*. Vintage Books, 1992.

Sandy, Mark. ""Cut by Rainbow": Tales, Tellers, and Reimagining Wordsworth's Pastoral Poetics in Toni Morrison's "Beloved" and "A Mercy."" *MELUS*, vol. 36, no. 2, Summer 2011, pp. 35-51.

Strehle, Susan. ""I Am a Thing Apart": Toni Morrison, A Mercy, and American Exceptionalism." *Critique: Studies in Contemporary Fiction*, vol 54, no. 2, April 2013, pp. 109-123.

Tally, Justine. "Contextualizing Toni Morrison's Ninth Novel: What Mercy? Why Now?" In Toni Morrison's *A Mercy: Critical Approaches*. Edited by Shirley A Stave and Justine Tally. Cambridge Scholars Publishing, 2011, pp. 63-84.

Wardi, Anissa. "The Politics of 'Home' In *A Mercy*." In Toni Morrison's *A Mercy: Critical Approaches*. Edited by Shirley A Stave and Justine Tally. Cambridge Scholars Publishing, 2011, pp. 23-41.

Willard, Mara. "Interrogating *A Mercy*: Faith, Fiction, and the Postsecular." *Christianity and Literature*, vol. 63, no. 4, Summer 2014, pp. 467-487.

CHAPTER 2

# Eurocentrism and African Cultural Disintegration

## Ideological Reflections from *Idea of Kawaida* and *The Bluest Eye*

Lehasa Moloi

> "We are dislocated, and having lost sight of ourselves in the mist of European decadence and madness, it becomes increasingly difficult for us to orient our lives in a positive and constructive manner"
>
> (Ama Mazama 2001, 388).

THE ADVENT of European colonial expedition, which began in the early 15th century and reached its apex during the 1884/85 Berlin Conference, formalised the physical scramble of the African continent to serve the interest of the competing European nations. The European colonial mission not only dismembered the physical environment of the continent of Africa, but it went further to inaugurate the enslavement of the African people, particularly, in the diaspora and the continent, and psychologically reconstructed the cosmology of African people to imagine themselves as Europeans. Ngugi wa Thiong'O (1986) defined what was unleashed by European imperialism as a 'cultural bomb' and elaborated on the long-term consequences in this eloquent manner:

> The effect of a cultural bomb is to annihilate a people's belief in their names, in their language, in their heritage of struggle, in their unity, in their capacities and ultimately in themselves. It makes them see their past as one wasteland of non-achievement and it makes them want to identify with that which is furthest removed from themselves; for instance, with other people's language rather than their own. It makes them identify with that which is decadent and reactionary, all those forces that would stop their own springs of life. It even plants serious doubts about moral rightness of struggle. Possibilities of triumph or victory are seen as remote, ridiculous dreams. The intended results are despair, despondency and a collective death-wish. Amidst this wasteland which it has created, imperialism presents itself as the cure and demands that the dependent sing hymns of praise with constant refrain: 'Theft is holy'
>
> (Ngugi wa Thiong'O 1986: 3).

Cultural disintegration is therefore, one of the key challenges faced by African people in their attempt to remember their lives against the colonial divisive culture which has disrupted their lives. Frantz Fanon, speaking from revolutionary struggle in Algeria and the study of colonialism in Africa and the world, points out the dual physical and cultural content of domination (1968, p. 210). He states that, in its very character, colonialism is organised and suppressive. Nonetheless, colonialism did not only impose its destructive cultural effects on the present imagination of its victims but extended itself to their conception of the future. In essence, it psychologically appropriated their thinking capabilities and disabled them from re-imagining themselves within their own historical and cultural terms. Moreover, Fanon (1968, p. 41) highlights that the colonial oppressor works to deny the culture of the oppressed who 'are declared insensitive to ethics; they represent not only the absence of values but negation of values' (Asante, 2009, p.30-31). Thus, colonialism and its underpinning ideology of White supremacy attacked the very foundation of what defines the Africans, that is their belief systems, identity and their worldviews and replaced these with European imputed identity and cultural norms.

Perhaps the critical challenge now faced by the African people is how they restore their own lives to live as functional citizens grounded within their own history and culture in their quest for liberation. This chapter aims to challenge the impact of Eurocentric culture and in particular, to reflect on how it has denied the ontology of the African people to think and retrieve their memory and to remold their lives on the grounds of their history and culture as a resource through their own agency. The first section interrogates Eurocentrism and its impact on African cultural disintegration, followed by introducing the concept of Kawaida as defined by Maulana Karenga and reflections made by Toni Morrison in her novel *The Bluest Eye* as a way to build resistance and unity as Africa searches for her identity.

## Eurocentrism and African cultural disintegration

Perhaps, the good starting point is to provide an explanation of what fundamentally constitutes Eurocentrism as a concept and interpretative metaparadigm for the explanation of social reality.

Amin (1989) describes Eurocentrism 'as one of the greatest ideological deformations of our time as it has falsely invented Europe to become the sole modern imaginary centre of the world and as the inventor of all positive human values. Joseph, Reddy and Chatterjee ((1990, p. 1) also highlight that ethnocentrism, of which Eurocentrism is the case in view, 'is the tendency to view one's own ethnic group and its social standards as the basis for evaluative judgements concerning the practices of others—with the implication that one views one's own standards as superior.' Thus, African people's concept of self became shaped by the unjust history of negation promoted by Europeans who did not have any regard for their humanity.

Eurocentrism has not only shaped the academic disciplines in African universities, which have functioned as satellites campuses to promote European epistemic superiority, but also extended itself to living experiences of African people, in particular—how they interpret and practice their spirituality. To be specific, the influence of Roman Catholicism and protestant evangelicalism as the key driving spiritual perspectives associated with Western modernity project. These perspectives in their attempt to offer spiritual salvation, have encouraged the African people to neglect their own spiritual practices in exchange for those taught by their colonial masters. Thus, African people were encouraged to abandon their own spiritual ethos as they were viewed as backward compared to the European 'higher' spiritual consciousness. Mlambo (2006, p. 165) highlights that western religion along with Eurocentric social sciences partnered in the dislocation of African minds to provide justification for colonialism as a noble undertaking. The Christian missionaries were used as colonial agents to transform the African belief system and to re-program the African minds to interpret their spiritual convictions in line with European spiritual cosmology.

To date, many practicing believers of African descent continue to abhor their own cultural practices in exchange for those imputed by their colonial missionaries. Ndlovu-Gatsheni (2018, p. 5) highlights that the negative consequences of Eurocentrism have been epistemicide, linguicides, culturicide, as well as alienation (exiling of indigenous people from their languages, histories, cultures and even from themselves). Thus, Eurocentrism affected all dimensions of African lives, be it political, social, economical, psychological and spiritual. The critical challenge facing Africans, therefore, is decolonizing themselves by taking power to redefine themselves as part of delinking from the oppressive culture.

Thus, cultural disintegration in Africa is attributable to the exogenous influence of Western imperialism through brute force. According to Mbakogu (2004, p. 38) cultural disintegration refers to the destabilization instituted when cultural changes go beyond the control of the people who are being colonized. The lasting violent colonial appropriation of Africa by invading European nations, made possible the dehumanization of African people, and in particular, facilitated the enslavement of the African people for economic benefits and extended itself through racial and cultural stereotyping (Viriri & Mungwini, 2010, p. 28). Asante (2014, p. 115) argues that the German historian, G.W.F Hegel, who never even set foot in Africa, projected Africans in negative terms in the Western social sciences. In his 1820 Lectures on History, Hegel argued that Africa should be forgotten because it was no part of history. The primary agenda of his work was geared towards inferiorizing humanity and the accomplishments of African people as a strategy to justify European desire to conquer the continent. As Viriri & Mungwini (2010, p. 29) argue that the process of colonial expropriation camouflaged itself as a civilizing and saving mission in order to hide the malicious intentions against Africans. This process deemed Africans as objects to be converted into desired European objects through the colonial education system. Indeed, this resulted into the invention of a European-made idea of Africa.

The colonial education system was used as a political tool to restructure the memory of African people, thus creating colonial subjects who must emulate their colonial masters. This resulted in Africans being moved farther away from their own history, culture and agency, and being infused with someone else's story. The violent historical experiences of Africa under colonization traumatized African brilliance and converted them into slaves who depended on their own self-imposed masters. In the light of these unfortunate circumstances, Sabelo Ndlovu-Gatsheni (2017) asked the necessary question: What does development/progress mean for a people struggling to emerge and free themselves from such inimical legacies of enslavement, colonialism, neo-colonialism, imperialism and underdevelopment? Indeed, this would require relocation of the Africans back to their own terms and would need them to delink from the Euro-oppressive culture and imposed knowledge systems, and be mentally decolonized to re-appreciate themselves and trust their own knowledge.

## Kawaida to revitalize African cultural value systems

Maulana Karenga, as a leading contemporary African American scholar and cultural theorist, conceptualized and introduced the concept of Kawaida as a redemptive communitarian philosophy, with the objective of regrounding the African people cross-continentally on the ethos of their African cultural foundations to dismantle colonial oppression. According to Karenga (1997, p. 17), the term 'Kawaida' is derived from the Kiswahili language and is translated by Karenga to denote 'customs,' suggesting 'inherited rules and principles which govern the way one thinks and acts in the world'. Accordingly, Karenga (2008, p. 4) defines Kawaida as a reconstructive cultural and communitarian philosophy and practice, focusing on culture and community as twin pillars of its intellectual and practical focus, framework and foundation. Within this framework, 'its fundamental thrust is to inspire, inform and sustain cultural revolution and national or communal liberation and new paradigm of being human in the world' (Karenga, 2008, p. 4). As per Asante, 'Karenga understood his own philosophical process as one that combines the elements of reason and tradition through facilitating and working out ideas and responses by shaping inherited traditions in the light of reasons and practical lessons' (Asante, 2009, p. 108). Karenga introduced his philosophy as an alternative way of knowing and interpreting social reality for people of African descent to overcome the oppressive Eurocentric culture that has denied them their right to express their cosmology. Given that European hegemony has been in full operation for 500 years since the rise of modern Europe, actively denying African people their right as part of human family to operate within their own cosmology. Kawaida, therefore, enters the debate to enrich the horizons of reason with the aim to grant African people the intellectual standpoint in the fight to re-emerge and assert their own agency.

Through the concept of Kawaida, Karenga seeks free exchange with other cultures in the world on an equal footing. He does not seek disengagement from the world, rather the right of the African people to speak. According to Karenga (2008, p. 5) until we Africans break the monopoly of oppression in our minds, liberation is not only impossible, but it's unthinkable. Asante (2009, p. 110) also emphasizes that culture is to people what oxygen is to the lungs. It is our breath of life, and if you are not breathing your own culture, then you are in fact breathing somebody else's culture. The concept of culture within this paper draws from Molefi Asante who defines culture as 'shared perceptions, attitudes, and predisposition that allows people to organize their experiences in a certain way' (Asante, 1990, p. 9). Therefore, the monumental task facing the African people as they seek to free themselves from Eurocentric cultural prison is to take refuge in their own historical and cultural terms.

Asante (2009, p. 109) highlights that there are four significant constituents to Karenga's definition of Kawaida; the first is that Kawaida is community related and connected in its make-up. Thus, Kawaida was not created as some separate, isolated, distant, or imaginary theory, rather it is organically attached to African communities worldwide. Secondly, Asante (2009: 109) affirms that Kawaida is not merely connected to the African communities in a static sense and by definition but rather by the context of the struggle. Thus, the Kawaida philosophy, the struggle for liberation of Africans is part of the definition of Kawaida. Thirdly, it involves an 'ongoing synthesis' in the sense that there are constant and consistent actions to create, mould, conceptualize, and articulate action based on the 'best of African thought and practice,' which reflects its pan-African character (Asante, 2009, p. 109). Lastly, Kawaida involves constant exchange with the world. To this effect, Asante (2009, p. 109) argues that 'Kawaida is neither separatist nor insular; it is, a philosophy that depends by definition on its ceaseless exchange with other peoples and philosophies of the world.' Like Afrocentricity, it does not seek to become a totalizing voice on culture, rather it seeks equality within the world in which Africans have been deprived to express, to grant them the avenue to speak from their cultural location. In view of Kawaida, the main problem is the cultural disintegration of Africans created throughout the history of their domination by Europe. As an expression of centrism, it demands Africans to be grounded in their ways of life, thus granting them a voice to speak and to belong as affirmed human beings. Karenga's intent is to understand the social, psychological, and moral location of Africans and attempt to change the strategies for transforming our conditions (Asante, 2009, p. 9).

It is important to note that Kawaida was influenced by three main ancient African cultures, namely, Zulu, which is from the Southern part of the African continent, Yoruba, which is from West Africa, and the Kemetic culture, which is from the ancient Northern part of Africa (Egypt). According to Asante (2009, p. 145), 'All these three cultures reflect something quite ancient and also rather valuable in the nature of culture as an instrument of revivification or renaissance.' However, it is important to note and understand that the African culture is not only limited to these three cultures, but they are mainly used to understand Karenga's sources of intervention in the reconstruction of African culture in the USA and globally. From the three cultures Karenga was able to formulate the Nguzo Saba (seven principles of Kwanzaa), namely, Umoja (Unity), Kujiichagulia (Self-determination), Ujima (Collective work and responsibility), Ujamaa (Cooperative economics), Nia (Purpose), Kuumba (Creativity) and Imani (Faith), which are based on communitarian values in ancient African societies (Asante, 2009, p. 169). Thus, the African people cannot live freely in the world without expressing their own cosmology but they will continue to regurgitate the imputed false consciousness, which serves their cultural dislocation. As such, Karenga (2008) believes that Africans can only deactivate the 'cultural dislocation' and liberate themselves only if they draw from their history the best practices, thus, he sees historical responsibility as an emancipatory charge to:

> Empty our minds and hearts of the toxic residue of racism, restore our historical memory and regain the historical initiative in determining our destiny and daily lives. For only with such an uninfected, healthy, wholesome self-understanding and self-assertion in the world can we truly know our past and honor it, engage our present and improve it in dignity-affirming and life-enhancing ways worthy of the name and history of Africans. (Karenga, 2008, p. 20)

For this reason, it is important to rewind the minds of the oppressed to reconnect them to their lost traditions as a way to empower themselves from marginalisation. Kawaida as a revolutionary intellectual and cultural critique has given many students of African descent the hope they need to stand on their own feet and to trust their own knowledge and voice in a world that has sought to diminish their natural flair towards excellence. By pinpointing the dilemma created by colonial scholarship to reproduce African people as imbeciles who have contributed nothing but the despotic civilizations in comparison to the so-called great nations of Europe. This negative portrayal of Africans through European historians was nothing other than an attempt to dehumanize Africans. Thus, removing them from the zone of humanity into the zone of sub-human savages who must rely on the tutelage of Europeans. Asante (1998:8) laments that

> ...if there is anything Africans have lost under European domination, it is their cultural centeredness; that is, we have been moved from our own platforms. This means we cannot truly be ourselves or know our potential since we exist in a borrowed space and have become the spectators of a show that defines us without our own input.

This implies that without an understanding of our historical past, we remain trapped as objects of European experimentation. Against this historical and cultural dislocation anomaly, Kawaida, therefore, proposes that Africans must be restored to and placed within their own historical and cultural setting as a way to overcome their de-centredness and disorientation. It is only when African people become fully restored, they can function fully to claim their own destiny.

## Toni Morrison's reflections on identity, race and gender in *The Bluest Eye*

Having reflected on the dilemma that Eurocentrism has created upon Africans in their quest for liberation, in this section, I reflect on the ideas expressed by Toni Morrison on how to rebuild the victorious consciousness among Africans. While Maulana Karenga has provided the intellectual framing through which to understand how the African cultural crisis has dislocated their self-concept, and disabled them to interpret their social realities from their own terms; Toni Morrison through her novel *The Bluest Eye* provides an elaboration in the form of creative writing to unmask how Eurocentric colonial culture has shaped African perception of themselves. I do not seek to exhaustively deal with every aspect of her novel rather I seek to provide the synopsis of how the novel helps to unmask societal decay through exposing how racism shapes African perceptions of themselves. Toni Morrison's *The Bluest Eye*, published in 1970, narrates the story of a little African American girl Pecola who is shattered by feelings of self-loathing and rejection from those around her. *The Bluest Eye* is a remonstration against the adoption of foreign beauty standards as a positive and universal value, and the agenda of the novelist through this book aims to reconstruct healthy identities through the reconstruction of culture and tradition as a resource to rebuild the healthy and positive identities (Gomes, 2016). Through her novel, Toni Morrison resuscitates discussions around themes such as identity, gender and race, in order to establish a dialogue within the African American scenery during the 1960s debates over such subjects. The internalization of racism created in Pecola the desire to have blue eyes as an epitome of beauty, thus eradicating her inferiority. Pecola's struggles with her visible body can be seen in the passage in which she wishes she could make it disappear:

> 'Please, God,' she whispered into the palm of her hand. 'Please make me disappear.' She squeezed her eyes shut. Little parts of her body faded away. Now slowly, now with a rush. Slowly again. Her fingers went, one by one; then her arms disappeared all the way to the elbows. Her feet now. Yes, that was good. The legs all at once. It was hardest above the thighs. She had to be real still and pull. Her stomach would not go. But finally, it, too, went away. Then her chest, her neck. The face was hard, too. Almost done, almost. Only her tight, tight eyes were left. They were always left. (The Bluest Eye, 1999).

From this quote, it is clear how inferiority complex makes one desire to become what one is not, in order to fit into the established false notions of beauty. Pecola's prayer for blue eyes as expressed in the novel shows how deeply deformed her identity and self-appreciation is, such that she desires to be more like Temple, Jane or the Fischer girl who are presented as the epitome of beauty standards. In that way, maybe, Pecola hopes she may come to be loved (Gomes, 2016, p. 25). After praying in the church, the young girl believes she has acquired blue eyes. Even though she believes she has acquired blue eyes after praying she still does not seem to be fulfilled, as expressed in the following quote:

> Please. If there is somebody with bluer eyes than mine, then maybe there is somebody with the bluest eyes. The bluest eyes in the whole world.

> That's just too bad, isn't it?
> Please help me look.
> But suppose my eyes aren't blue enough?
> Blue enough for what? Blue enough for...I don't know.
> Blue enough for something. Blue enough...for you!
> I'm not going to play with you anymore.
> Oh. Don't leave me.
> Yes. I am.
> Why? Are you mad at me?
> Yes.
> Because my eyes aren't blue enough? Because I don't have the bluest eyes?
> No. Because you're acting silly.
> Don't go. Don't leave me. Will you come back if I get them?
> Get what?
> The bluest eyes. Will you come back then?
> Of course, I will. I'm just going away for a little while.
> You promise?
> Sure. I'll be back. Right before your very eyes. (The Bluest Eye, 1999, pp. 201-202)

Without a doubt, as can be noticed in this quote, the very notion of what beautiful means, remains colonised within the dictates of Whiteness as a philosophical construct. Toni Morrison suggests that the very concept of beauty as seen through the lenses of Whiteness is harmful and exclusionary (Gomes, 2016). According to Du Bois (1903) because of the complications of the racist society, the African people suffer from 'double consciousness' (two warring souls in one dark body) as an expression of identity chaos that befalls them because of enslavement. For Molefi Asante (2007, p. 158) this condition is called 'tortured consciousness', as a result of African Americans being magnetized by White privilege and thus, experiencing pangs of self-hatred.

Therefore, Toni Morrison in the novel argues that instead of promoting just the idea that blackness be considered beautiful, she proposes that the valorisation of Africans should originate from placing importance on their culture, traditions and connection to the community as a way to find healing from the effects of tortured consciousness. Her views affirm Maulana Karenga's notion of Kawaida and the significance of cultural revolution to overcome cultural disintegration created through Eurocentric colonisation of terms. Toni Morrison believes that the only way African women can overcome their distorted self-concept because of the White dominant culture is to be restored to their cultural traditions. Pecola's socio-economic conditions meant that she is viewed as black and ugly and her only hope was to dream of becoming white. This is the situation everywhere in the world where African people are oppressed. They see themselves as unworthy and have a desire to become white in order to escape their conditions. What seems clear in both Toni Morrison and Maulana Karenga's idea of Kawaida is the need for relocating African communities within their own culture as a way to find healing. Without relocating as African people to our own terms, we will continue to rely on those who define us, and as such we will not be fully equipped to fulfil our destiny.

## Conclusion

This paper provided an Afrocentric conceptual intervention and reflected on the impact of Eurocentrism on African cultural crisis through the reconstruction of African identities and the production of African American inferiority complex syndrome. The paper reflected the work of two renowned African American scholars and activists, namely, Maulana Karenga's idea of *Kawaida* and Toni Morrison's reflections on identity, race and gender as captured in her novel *The Bluest Eye*, with an objective to address the cultural crisis among the African people cross-continentally. The primary emphasis was on the significance of re-grounding African people within their own cultural ethos as a base from which to reconstruct their identities to overcome Eurocentric oppressive and divisive culture. The paper was segmented into the following three sections. The first section provided an analysis of what constitutes Eurocentrism as a concept and as a practise and how it has negatively contributed to the cultural disintegration among Africans. Secondly, the paper deployed Maulana Karenga's concept of *Kawaida* as a useful and relevant Afrocentric cultural philosophy to revitalize African cultural ethos with an aim to debunk Eurocentrism. Lastly, the paper reflected on the lesson from Toni Morrison's novel on how to build wholesome, healthy identities by suggesting relocation of Africans to their culture and traditions, in an attempt to re-affirm the significance of African resistance against oppression.

## Works Cited

Amin, S. Eurocentrism. New York, NY: Monthly Review Press, 1989.

Asante, M.K. *The Afrocentric Idea* (revised and expanded edition). Philadelphia, PA: Temple University Press, 1998.

Asante, M.K. *Afrocentricity: The Theory of Social Change* (Revised and expanded). Chicago, IL: African American Images, 2003.

Asante, M.K. *An Afrocentric Manifesto: Toward an African Renaissance.* Cambridge & Oxford: Polity Press, 2007.

Asante, M.K. *Maulana Karenga: An Intellectual Portrait.* Cambridge, UK. Polity Press, 2009.

Bhebe, N. M. 2000. "Colonial Stultification of African Science and Technology and the Abuse of African Culture". In Viriri, A and Mungwini, P. 2010. African cosmology and the duality of Western hegemony: the search for African Identity. *Journal of Pan African Studies*, vol 3, no. 6, March, pp. 27-42.

Du Bois, W.E.B. *The Souls of Black Folk: Essays and Sketches.* Chicago, IL: Lawrence Hill, 1903.

Gomes, R. R. M. Identity, Race and Gender in Toni Morrison's The Bluest Eye. Available at: www.researchgate.net (accessed on 01/02/2021), 2016.

Joseph, G. G, Reddy, V and Searle-Chatterjee, M. *Eurocentrism in the Social Sciences. Race & Class*, vol. 31, no. 4, 1990.

Karenga, M. *Kawaida and Questions of Life and Struggle: African American, Pan-African and Global Issues.* Los Angeles: University of Sankore Press, 2008.

Mazama, A. 2001. *The Afrocentric paradigm: Contours and definitions. Journal of Black Studies,* vol. 31, no. 4, 2001, pp. 387-405.

Mazama, A. 2014. *Afrocentricity and the Critical Question of African Agency.* [Online] Available at https://www.dyabukam.com/index.php/en/knowledge/ philosophy/item/136-afrocentricity (Accessed: 19 January 2018).

Mbakogu, I.A. 2004. Is there really a relationship between culture and development? *Anthropology*, vol. 6, no. 1, pp. 37-43.

Mlambo, A. S. "Western Social Sciences and Africa: The Domination and Marginalisation of a Continent." *African Sociological Review*, vol. 10, no. 1, 2006, pp. 161-179.

Monteiro-Ferreira, A. *The demise of the Inhumane: Afrocentricity, Modernism, and Postmodernism.* Albany, NY: Sunny Press, 2014.

Morrison, T. The Bluest Eye. London: Vintage Books, 1999.

Ndlovu-Gatsheni, S.J. "The African idea of development." In Binns, T., Lynch, K. and Nels, E. (eds.), *Routledge Handbook of African Development*, pp. 1-16. London: Routledge, 2017.

Ndlovu-Gatsheni, S.J. *Epistemic Freedom in Africa: Deprovincialization and Decolonization.* London: Routledge, 2018.

Ngugi wa Thiong'o. *Decolonizing the Mind: The Politics of Language in African Literature.* Oxford: James Currey, 1986.

Viriri, A. and Mungwini, P. African cosmology and the duality of Western hegemony: the search for African Identity. *Journal of Pan African Studies*, vol. 3, no. 6, March 2010, pp. 27-42.

CHAPTER 3

# Post What ? The Disarticulation of Post-racial Discourse

Abdelkader Ben Rhit

## Introduction

'THOSE WHITE things have taken all I had or dreamed and broke my heartstrings too. There is no bad luck in the world but White folks,' Baby Suggs, a character in Morrison's *Beloved* says to her daughter Sethe. (*Beloved* 89) Suggs's words encapsulate the African Americans' dilemma, the centuries of oppression, racism, and traumatic experiences they have been through since the Middle Passage at the hands of White people. In the twenty-first century and in the purported 'post-racial' America, racial injustice and widespread murdering and other forms of violence are continuing against the Afro-Americans. Slavery has officially ended after all the abolitionist, Civil Rights and Liberation Movements but the Black people are still physically and psychologically oppressed in America.

The Black Lives Matter (BLM) international social movement, which was formed in the United States in 2013, is dedicated to fighting racism and violence against the African Americans, especially in the form of police brutality. It condemns the unjust murdering of Black people by police and it demands that society value the lives and humanity of Black people as much as it values the lives and humanity of White people (*Britannica*). 'Were [Morrison] still alive, she undoubtedly would have thrown her unequivocal support behind the BLM movement and galvanized everyone,' argues Konomi Ara who goes on to say, 'but Morrison would have supported the cause only through her writing' (qtd. in *The Asahi Shimbun*). Morrison has devoted her life and writings to defend the rights of the marginalized and voiceless African Americans.

The now 'free' Afro-Americans are still subject to various forms of oppression. Their quest for freedom is still an ongoing phenomenon in America. African Americans 'bear daily the burdensome trace of violence as "a tax to pay" for their existence.' Evidence is exceedingly spattered on television screens, leaving us shackled, muted by inexpressible shock and awe (Ben Beya 86). Reading Morrison's fictional writings within the context of the Black Lives Matter protests, this chapter analyzes Morrison's female protagonists' traumatic experiences, their endurance and their quest for freedom. It focuses on the fact that these very unbearable conditions reveal the characters' basic nature as heroines coming to terms with the real meaning of their existence. It shows how every character bears the weight of responsibility for his own life and at last finds a way of lifting him up from his own and other's guilt to progresses and glory.

The idea of freedom, which is central in Morrison novels, has been powerfully affected by slavery, racism, injustice and inequality in the American society. Almost all Morrison's novels have been remarkable for their divergent routes in the quest for freedom. Like the Black Lives Matter protests, Morrison's novels have attempted to shake White people's collective memories out of dis-remembrance of coloured lives and to demand accountability from abusers. The *Bluest Eye, Sula, Song of Solomon, Tar Baby, and Beloved* are novels of protest against White racism, sexism, patriarchy and slavery. They are songs for the 'disremembered and unaccounted for' (*Beloved* 274) because they delineate the African American female protagonists' journey of struggle for survival, their protest against the various forms of oppression they have been subject to by both the Americans and the African Americans, and finally their freedom and assertion of their Black selves. Morrison's women's quest for freedom and for a sense of self emanate from excruciating experiences of marginalisation and abuse. Suffering for the African American women is empowering rather than paralysing. Morrison asserts, 'what is heroic that's the way I know why such people survive' and it's this 'way' and this 'why' that this chapter explores at length (Guthrie 181).

## Commitment and Black Feminism in Morrison's Novels

Morrison's novels can be qualified as literature of commitment because of their ideological or political stance. She writes about the predicament of the entire Black race—both men and women 'celebrating the strengths of African American women against the heavy odds of racism and sexism by developing the necessary political, social and aesthetic consciousness' (Dastageer 21). She supports strongly the cause of the Black men and women. Her writings, fictional and non-fictional, demonstrate that she writes for the liberation of her fellow African American in America.

For Morrison, writing fiction is her weapon to bear witness to the Black people's traumatic experiences and to give them voice. She gives full support to the African American women who were the most affected by the triple jeopardy of racism, sexism, and classism. Her novels include traces of the Black Feminism movement though the movement and theory came much later. The significance of empowerment, the legacy of struggle, the quest for freedom, which are the core themes of Black Feminism, are present in her writings. Her novels are mainly about African American women, their traumas, their struggle for survival and freedom from the perils of racial degeneracy and cultural inferiority. African American women in America have been victimized because of their race, gender and class (Chapagain 116). Their traumatic psychological condition is caused by racism, sexism, and classism.

Morrison's novels function as political and social commentary. For her, 'the function of the novel is... to illuminate and engage with social and cultural conflicts and do justice to their complexities' (Lister 13). She was 'conscious of the nature of the African's dilemma, the crisis of the African personality, its cause and effects', and she had 'increasing commitment to help solve it in terms of fictional art, thereby combining her political consciousness with aesthetic sensibility' (Dastageer 21). As a Black feminist, Morrison fought against racism, sexism, and gender stereotypes through her fictional and non-fictional works. Black feminism 'is not simply a struggle to end male chauvinism or a movement to ensure that women will have equal rights with men; it is a commitment to eradicate the ideology of domination that permeates the Western culture on various levels: sex, race, and class...' (Hooks 194). Black feminism has focused on other issues, such as race, which was not addressed by classic feminism.

Wang explained that 'Morrison's feminism is most appealing to [her] for she accounts not only gender but also race and class' (Wu 406). All female characters Pecola, Sula, Jadine, Pilate and Sethe are victims of race, class and gender in different ways. Though, Morrison wrote about the effects of slavery on the psyche of the African American women it is portrayed from various perspectives, from racism, sexism and classism and the multi-faceted sufferings a African American woman has to undergo during the era of slavery and also in the post slavery era. The next paragraphs examine Morrison's representation of African American females' suffering and journey to attain freedom and discover their identities.

## Stories of Pain: Trauma and Struggle for Survival and Freedom

In the selected novels, *The Bluest Eye*, *Sula*, *Tar Baby*, *Song of Solomon*, and *Beloved*, Morrison narrates her female protagonists' painful experiences and their attempt to free themselves from the various forms of oppression perpetrated by the White and Black people. Her portrayal shows the impact of racism, patriarchy, and classism on the shaping of the heroines' identities and their quest for freedom. Her tales of pain bear witness to the traumas faced by African American female protagonists, because of their race, gender and class in America and show their evolving consciousness leading to their freedom from the shackles of slavery, racism, sexism, and classism.

*The Bluest Eye*, Morrison's first novel, traces the adversities and painful experiences of a African American girl named

Pecola who yearns to have blue eyes, which she thinks, will end her grief and bring her the love she longs for from her hate-filled family, sarcastically named Breedlove. In this novel, the traumatic suffering of Pecola is due to the White standards of beauty. Being female and colored are the causes of Pecola's suffering. Her yearning for White beauty standard of blue eyes is impossible to meet. Being poor is another reason for her oppressive condition. As Claudia puts it, 'Being a minority in both caste and class we moved about on the helm of life' (*The Bluest Eye* 11). The words of Minha Mae 'to be female in this place is to be an open wound that cannot heal. Even if scars form, the festering is ever below' (*A Mercy* 163) is what trauma is all about.

Pecola is subject to various forms of oppression from both White and African American people alike. She 'is the epitome of the victim in a world that reduces persons to objects and then makes them feel inferior as objects' (Davis 330). There are many instances where Pecola is treated in a racist manner. For example, Yacobowski, for instance, does not want contact with Pecola because of her blackness. Pecola 'has seen it lurking in the eyes of all White people. So, the distaste must be for her, her blackness' (*The Bluest Eye* 49). Yacobowski evades touching Pecola's hands when she hands over the money for the chocolate she buys. He 'hesitates, not wanting to touch her hand' (*The Bluest Eye* 49). The ultimate traumatic experience for Pecola is being raped by her own father, Cholly.

In her search for freedom, Pecola has failed to free herself from the White standards of beauty. Her failure to see the beauty in her makes her suffer from low self-esteem. Unlike Pecola, Claudia and her sister are satisfied and happy with their difference, their blackness. Claudia says: 'Guileless and without vanity, we were still in love with ourselves then we felt comfortable in our skins, enjoyed the news that our senses released to us, admired our dirt, cultivated our scars, and couldn't comprehend this unworthiness' (*The Bluest Eye* 74). By enjoying their colour and feeling at ease with their skins, Claudia and her sister not only question their 'unworthiness' and fight against the established White ideologies but also manage to survive and coexist within the white milieu. One should understand that beauty is not in the colour of the skin and being black is only an alternative condition of existence in the world rather than a sign of inferiority. Morrison's message, illustrated through Pecola and Claudia, is that Black people should be content with their blackness and they should not give up fighting to establish themselves in an alien and hostile environment because it is the only way to find peace and happiness.

In *Sula*, the female protagonist Sula tries very hard to free herself in a hostile and oppressive world. She is victimized by sexism and racism inflicted on her by the American society. Sula's exposure to multiple traumatic events, such as the death of her mother and father, causing the death of Chicken Little, losing Nel's friendship, being black and abandoned by Ajax, has a deep psychological impact on her. Jill Matus observes that Sula is haunted by 'sorrow and pain' (63). 'Traumatic narratives are about the failed attempts to free oneself, the impossibility of escape' (Ben Beya 98). Morrison clarifies, 'freeing yourself was one thing; claiming ownership of that freed self was another' (*Beloved* 95), which means that the entanglement remains intact even after freeing oneself. The latter creates the 'ethical responsibility' to tell. To witness is to hear history from the perspective of the traumatized subject" (Ben Beya 98). Morrison gives Sula a space and voice to tell her painful story. The novel depicts the heroine's journey in the quest for freedom and a meaningful identity in a world of growing hostility.

Sula's extreme emotional impulses and her strange, strong, and independent character startles the community in which she lives. These are shown in her rejection of all behavioural standards and values of society and her attempts to create her own standards. She rejects the limitations of institutions of marriage and motherhood by leaving the Bottom and going away seeking emotional and physical freedom from society's order and control. Anne Mickelson portrayed her as the rebel, 'who exceeds boundaries, creates excitement, tries to break free of encroachment of external cultural forces, and challenges destiny' (129). To Eva's question 'when you gone to get married? You need to have some babies. It'll settle you', Sula replies, 'I don't want to make somebody else. I want to make myself' (*Sula* 92). Unlike Eva who sacrifices her physical freedom for economic freedom and Nel who accommodates herself to the protection of marriage, Sula resists both sacrifice and accommodation.

Sula's freedom from the signifiers of racial degeneracy, from fear and her tough and rebellious character are reasons behind her self-empowerment. Sula 'was completely free of ambition, with no affection for money, property or things, no greed, no desire to command attention or compliments—no ego. For that reason, she felt no compulsion to verify herself - be consistent with herself ... like any artist with no art form…' (*Sula* 119-121). Here again, Morrison portrays Sula as a revolutionary character to be followed by oppressed women who must revolt against their oppressors who block their ways to freedom.

Morrison's female protagonists try to gain their freedom and assert their Black identity by protesting against the white and black oppressive forces. Though all the female protagonists are oppressed by the male characters, only a few women characters like Pilate Dead, Corinthians and Lina in *Song of Solomon* and Jadine and Ondine in *Tar Baby* protest against their oppressors. Pilate's loss of her mother since her birth and being deprived of a loving father since twelve have filled her life with grief. The disenchanted memories of her early childhood agonize and alienate Pilate. However, she is able to survive in the Black American society by creating a world of her own. She manages to face these adversities and carves out a space of her own. Similarly, Corinthians attempts to assert her Black identity by having a job and leaving the hostile environment in which she lives.

In *Tar Baby*, Jadine Childs's trauma is due to her double consciousness, her desire to be loyal to both American and African American cultures. She forgets her ancestry; she is mad about New York and the white culture. She has a strong will and she wants her economic freedom. Being free and independent is what matters most for Jadine. She is ready to drop anybody who blocks her way to freedom even the person she loves very much. Similarly, Ondine, who is a servant, values her freedom and independence. She dares to give her mistress a smack in her husband's presence when she abused her. Jadine and Ondine are rebels who raise their voice of protest both against White and African American oppressors.

Although she works as a model in Europe, Jadine knows that she is neither accepted in the White society nor in the

African American society. She is rejected by both the White and African American communities. For Jadine, economic success is her way to equality with the Whites. Unlike Jadine, Son thinks that one must understand one's history first and one should not forget one's own culture. Jadine values her freedom and independence. She rebels against her blackness and she yearns for an independent free self. Patrick Bjork argues that Jadine's 'acceptance of disconnection from a cultural heritage serve as an indictment against her for denying the cultural knowledge that may further empower her' (138). Jadine represents the new African American youth who are indoctrinated by the formal education and the dominant values of White America.

Jadine is able to manage the oppressive class system but she fails to value her own culture and tradition. She represents Morrison's emancipated new woman, who breaks the age-old traditions and conventions set up by patriarchy, race, gender and class bias. She succeeds to live a life free of race, gender and class but she fails to resolve her inner conflict about her racial identity. This may be taken as Morrison's suggestion that for an African American female to attain a wholesome personality she should have clear understanding of her history, culture, and identity.

As a trauma narrative, Morrison's fifth novel *Beloved* 'is framed around the necessity to tell the forceful commandment, to bear witness and to testify, confessing the truth of horror' (Ben Beya 96). *Beloved* narrates the historical trauma of slavery, which is the most agonizing period in the Black people's history. The novel is a haunting blend of the past and present traumatic experiences of Sethe, a female freedom seeker. As Morrison says, 'this was not a book about the institution—Slavery with a capital S. It was about these anonymous people called slaves.

What they do to keep on, how they make a life, what they're willing to risk, however long it lasts, in order to relate to one another' (Angelo 257). Sethe kills her infant to free her from the shackles of slavery, a haunting event which causes her sense of guilt and grief. For Ranveer, Sethe 'is fated, but she tries to liberate herself and her children from this given fate' (Ranveer 43). Morrison dares to speak out the unspeakable and rips the veil on the hidden realities of sore ordeals. She examines the deep physical and psychological wounds of slavery and recalls Sethe's bold flight to freedom in Ohio in 1855. Freedom, as Paul D's and Sethe's painful stories illustrate, 'is to get to a place where you could love anything you chose—not to need permission for desire' (*Beloved* 162).

Sethe is in constant search for freedom. She is deprived of her mother's milk as a child and of a proper marriage when she is young. Her breast milk is taken from her by force and given to her master. She has been struggling for survival and protesting against the horrors of slavery. Sethe's plan to escape from her White master's house and her decision to marry Halle are her first steps towards gaining freedom and establishing her identity. Her tough decision to kill her own children in order to free her from the shackles of slavery signify her strong desire for a life free of bondage. Similarly, Denver, Sethe's second daughter, becomes highly independent and strong, supporting her mother till the end. Her bravery and responsibility help her protest against her past oppressed life and save her family from ruin. She has become a free being interacting freely with members of her community. Being the only remaining child of Sethe, Denver represents the future. The recollection and recreation of Sethe's repressed memories 'are essential to her recovery' (Krumholz 395). Memory is essential for her to achieve her freedom.

## Conclusion

To conclude, Morrison's selected novels portray different phases in the lives of Afro-Americans showing their journeys towards freedom. Pecola, in *The Bluest Eye*, Sula in *Sula*, Pilate in *Song of Solomon*, Jadine in *Tar Baby* and Sethe and Denver in *Beloved* are examples that illustrate the atrocities perpetrated on the African Americans by the White American institutions and their attempt to free themselves from the various forms of oppression inflicted on them. African American women have been victims of slavery, sexism, racism and classism. These are the problems that the Black females confront even today. Morrison's novels disarticulate the post-racial discourse in America. They offer a harsh critique of the American system of racism, sexism, and classism. They expose issues of race and how the American society has denied African Americans' freedom and racial identity.

In Morrison's novels, there are explicit messages to the Black community as a whole. Her first message is that the Black people must blend their past memories and experiences into their present lives so that they can truly demand their freedom. Although freedom is a personal dream in the first place, it converts to nothing if isolated from the more comprehensive collective communal vision.

The second message is the African American's need to purify themselves from whiteness. For an African American woman/man to acquire an identity, s/he must first purify herself/himself from 'whiteness'. To use DuBois's words 'to attain his place in the world, he must be himself, and not another' (20). S/he should be convinced that a new other self is to be created. Yet, s/he should realize that it is only herself/himself who can do it.

The third message is the importance of wholeness between men and women as members of one race. In order to reach one's dream of freedom, men and women should act as members of one race. The fourth message is to love one's flesh. This is clear, for instance, in Baby Suggs's advice to ex-slaves to 'Love your hands! Love them. Raise them up and kiss them. Touch others with them, pat them together, stroke them on your face 'cause they don't love that either. [...] hear me now, love your heart. For this is the prize' (*Beloved* 89). The black flesh that the Whites despise should be a sign of pride rather than one of shame.

The fifth message is of love and solidarity. All African American women should come together as one class to gain their freedom and discover their own identities through their bonding with one another. Here Morrison echoes James Baldwin definition of the word 'integration' which denotes that 'we, with love, shall force our brothers to see themselves as they are, to cease fleeing from reality and begin to change it' (23). The sixth message is to assume responsibility, which for Morrison is very important in molding an identity. For her, freedom and responsibility are inextricably intertwined. She tells Gloria Naylor, 'The point is that freedom is choosing your responsibility. It's not having no responsibilities; it's choosing the ones you want' (Naylor 16). Responsibility is a pre-condition that 'freedom' necessitates; it prepares people for their new selves. It is only when people 're-connect' themselves to their community that is ruled by love, a clear understanding of one's history, solidarity, and responsibility, either personal or communal, that they can reach their freedom.

## Works Cited

Baldwin, James. *The Fire Next Time.* Vintage, 2013.

Ben Beya, Abdennebi. "The Question of Reading Traumatic Testimony: Jones's *Corregidora* and Morrison's *Beloved.*" *Alif: Journal of Comparative Poetics*, vol. 30, 2010, pp. 85-109.

Bjork, Patrick Bryce. *The Novels of Toni Morrison: The Search for Self and Place within the Community.* New York: Peter Lang. 1992.

Bonnie Angelo, "The Pain of Being Black: An Interview with Toni Morrison," in *Conversations with Toni Morrison*, edited by Danielle Taylor-Guthrie, Jackson: University of Mississippi Press, 1994.

Britannica, The Editors of Encyclopaedia. "Black Lives Matter". *Encyclopedia Britannica*, 13 Aug. 2020, https://www.britannica.com/topic/Black-Lives-Matter. Accessed 24 May 2021.

Chapagain, Rajendra Prasad. "African American Women, Racism and Triple Oppression." *Interdisciplinary Journal of Management and Social Sciences*, vol. 1.1, 2020, pp. 113-117.

Dastageer, A. *The Struggle for Survival to the Joy of Liberation a Study of the Evolution of Black Female Consciousness in the Novels of Toni Morrison.* 2016. Bharathidasan University, PhD Dissertation. http://hdl.handle.net/10603/117427.

Davis, Cynthia A. "Self, Society, and Myth in Toni Morrison's Fiction." *Contemporary Literature*, vol. 23, no. 3, 1982, pp. 323-342. *JSTOR*, www.jstor.org/stable/1208158. Accessed 24 May 2021.

Du Bois, W. E. B. *The Souls of Black Folk.* New York: Everyman's Liberary/knopf, 1993.

Guthrie, T Danille.ed. *Conversations with Toni Morrison.* Jackson:

University Press of Mississippi, 1994.

Hooks, Bell. *Ain't IA Woman: Black Women and Feminism.* New York: Routledge, 2014.

Konomi, Ara. "Vox Populi: Reading Toni Morrison offers insight into Black Lives Matter." asahi.com, The Asahi Shimbun, 2020/08/11/ http://www.asahi.com/ajw/articles/13625842. Accessed 28 May 2021.

Krumholz, Linda. "The Ghosts of Slavery: Historical Recovery in Toni Morrison's *Beloved.*" *African American Review*, vol. 26, no. 1, Spring 1992, pp. 395- 408.

Lister, Rachel. *Reading Toni Morrison.* Santa Barbara, CA: Greenwood, 2009.

Matus, Jill. *Toni Morrison.* Manchester and New York: Manchester University Press, 1998.

Mickelson, Anne Z. *Reaching Out: Sensitivity and Order in Recent American Fiction by Women.* Metuchen, NJ: Scarecrow Press, 1979.

Morrison, Toni. *The Bluest Eye.* London: Pan, 1970.

---. *Sula.* New York: Vintage International, 2004.

---. *Song of Solomon*, London: Pan, 1977.

---. *Tar Baby.* London: Pan, 1981.

---. *Beloved.* New York: Signet, 1987.

---. *A Mercy.* London: Vintage Books, 2010.

Naylor, Gloria. *Conversations with Gloria Naylor.* Univ. Press of Mississippi, 2004.

Ranveer, Kashinath. *Black Feminist Consciousness: A Study of Black Women Writers*, Printwell, Jaipur: 1995.

Wu, Hui. "Post-Mao Chinese Literary Women's Rhetoric Revisited: A Case for an Enlightened Feminist Rhetorical Theory." *College English*, vol. 72, no. 4, 2010, pp. 406-423.

SECTION TWO

# BODY, RELATIONS AND HUMANISM

CHAPTER 4

# The Female Body

## A Glance into *Beloved* and *Home*

Bhawana Pokharel

TONI MORRISON wrote the critically acclaimed *Beloved* in 1987. It won a Pulitzer Prize for fiction in 1993. The novel is based on the true story of a runaway slave who, at the point of recapture, kills her infant daughter in order to spare her a life of slavery. Likewise, *Home* was written in 2012 which depicts a traumatized Korean War veteran who encounters rupturing racism after returning home but later overcomes warfare apathy and his personal guilt of victimizing a girl by rescuing his sister from the hands of an abusive White medical practitioner.

In this chapter, we look into two of Morrison's novels namely *Beloved* and *Home* and discuss how women's bodies were treated in her time and how women characters in her novels underwent the derogation and fragmentation of their bodies. It explores how such physically and psychologically disintegrated females in the novels feel disconnected from themselves as well as from the community. The novels depict that women are forcefully splintered from their 'selves' by slavery and patriarchy.

Patriarchy always tends to have control over women's body as well as mind. Likewise, racism relegates women to the level of sexual objects. Hence the physical and sexual assault inflicted by patriarchy and racism casts a bodily and psychological fragmentation upon women. The chapter introduces and interrogates primarily into the maltreatment experiences of Cee and Sethe along with other women characters that render a fragmentation of their being and body and discusses how violated women eventually protest. They appeal for solidarity among women of their own community and engage in the process of healing.

Morrison wrote *Home* in 2012. On one hand, it is the story of Frank Money, a twentyfour-year old African American veteran of the Korean War. Having spent some of his life in an integrated Army, he returns home i.e., the United States from Korea and finds fragmented societies and people in his homeland. He had received an anonymous note urging him to go back to Atlanta, Georgia, his hometown. The note mentioned that his sister Cee was in need to rescue her life. A sense of urgency was embedded in the note as it warned him if he makes any delays, he may not be able to save his sister. Frank himself is shown to have been a sufferer. He has been going through post-traumatic stress disorder (PTSD) caused by the atrocities and the traumatic situations created by the war. He frequently 'lapses into episodes'; lately too, he had been hospitalized due to the recurrence of a compulsive mental situation. As his normal discharge from the hospital was not possible, for going to visit his sister, he had to escape from the mental institution for Atlanta. He reaches there in the nick of time, intrudes into the house of the doctor with caution and cleverness, and takes her back to their hometown. As the doctor was experimenting on her, using her womb to research for his medical obsession, Cee was in a pathetic condition physically. Owing to this reason, it is the story of Cee Money and the violation as well as betrayal to her body by the White male representative of the era i.e., Dr Beauregard Scott (*Home* 58), who is also the representative of the whole White race.

Likewise, *Beloved* contains a story of Sethe, an ex-slave whom the painful memories of the past haunt. She worked at Sweet Home. The torturous moments she underwent at this abode and during her escape from there are depicted very vividly by Morrison in this novel. As a slave woman she was treated brutally, raped and her motherly possession of her newly born daughter, Denver was stolen by the Schoolmaster and other males at Sweet Home. It is revealed from her reunion with Paul D after 18 years in the haunted house of Sethe that Halle turns mad witnessing the rape of his own wife. She spends a blissful life with Baby Suggs after her escape from the Sweet Home, but the reappearance of Schoolteacher makes her willing to kill her children to break the chain of slavery, however she becomes successful to kill only one of her daughters so that she will not have to go through the same fate of women's physical and sexual fragmentation. But it haunts her and makes her suffer even more throughout her life. It is not only Sethe, but other female characters namely Beloved, Denver and Baby Suggs, mother of Sethe and Ella who also suffer much primarily as they are women.

Fragmentation has pervaded women's condition throughout history. In Morrison's novels fragmentation emanates from the oppressive systems of patriarchy and racism. Patriarchy always tends to have control over women's body and mind. Likewise, racism relegates women to the level of sexual objects. The physical and sexual assault inflicted by patriarchy and racism casts a bodily and psychological fragmentation upon women. Morrison's *Beloved* implicitly illustrates the psychological and bodily fractures caused through the agency of slavery and patriarchy. Sethe, the protagonist, undergoes physical abuse and psychological sufferings through the institutionalized slavery and patriarchy. It leads her to life-long traumatic effects and literal abnormality in her action of killing her daughter. Eventually, such disintegration necessitates women's protest and solidarity for the sake of healing.

## Fragmentation: Forms and Modes

From time immemorial, human body has been made to connote feminine. The female or woman is also deemed and derogated as weak, immoral and decaying. Angela King notes, 'In the mind/ body dualism the body and mind are regarded as quite separate, the body is merely the crude container of mind...Man is mind and represents culture: the rational, unified, thinking subject; woman is body and represents nature: irrational, emotional and driven by instinct and physical need' (30). It is a fact that women are subjugated primarily through their bodies. The fragmented body emerges from various, often intersecting forms of oppression, including patriarchy and racism.

Violence against women and their fragmentation, both physical and psychological, often go simultaneously. According to S. L. Bartky, women in patriarchal societies undergo a kind of fragmentation 'by being too closely identified with [their body]...[their] entire being is identified with the body, a thing which...has been regarded as less inherently human than the mind or personality' (130). Bartky believes that through this fragmentation a woman is objectified, since her body is separated from her person and is thought as representing the woman (130). And it is usually done with patriarchy that operates through the system of social structures and practices always dominating, oppressing or exploiting women.

Patriarchy as a system involves the concern and control of the female body. It views female body as an object of sexual incitement and pleasure for males. In this regard, Fredrickson and Roberts say that the common thread running through all forms of sexual objectification is the experience of being treated as a body (or collection of body parts) valued predominantly for its use to (or consumption by) others (174).

Patriarchy often reduces the women to the status of mere instruments for male sexual gratification and as a site of exercising power. According to Bartky, 'woman must make herself "object and pre"' for the man. ... Woman lives her body as seen by another, by an anonymous patriarchal Other' (73). In patriarchy, 'sex' is considered as normative, and as Foucault has called it 'a regulatory ideal' (qtd. in Butler 1).

Butler affirms, '[S]ex... not only functions as a norm but is part of a regulatory practice that produces the bodies it governs, that is, whose regulatory force is made clear as a kind of productive power, the power to produce—demarcate, circulate, differentiate—the bodies it controls (1). Sex as a regulatory force is problematic and gives rise to oppression as well as struggle under patriarchy. As such, women are denied the ownership of themselves, their bodies leading to fragmentation. Patriarchal notion of hierarchal rule and coercive authority is the root cause of violence and thus, of fragmentation. Putting forth the radical feminist voice, bell hooks in her "Introduction" to the book, *Feminism for Everybody*, mentions that males as a group have and do benefit the most from patriarchy for it allows them to assume that they are superior to females and should rule over them or they must to do it to keep patriarchy intact.

The ease that the long held system of patriarchy locates male at, is liable also to result into women's fragmentation at different levels and forms. Fragmentation of women and violence against them often stems from the domesticity and familial relation of men and women. Though violence against women is often the consequence of the exercise of power by the patriarch, hooks also indicates that males are not the only people who accept, condone and perpetuate violence, but also who create a culture of violence (65). The most important is the patriarchal thinking that needs to be changed both by men and women.

Racism, as another significant cause for bodily and psychological fragmentation, has a grave impact upon women's lives. For many enslaved African Americans, one of the cruelest hardships they endured was sexual abuse by the slaveholders, overseers and other Whites who had complete control over them. Human beings tend to function best as an integrated whole psychologically.

Out of that sense of wholeness and integrity, emerge meaning, purpose, value, belief, identity and wisdom. But the fragmentation that accompanies traumatic experiences degrades this integration, and impedes maximum performance in a variety of ways (Bloom 10) which might often be seen as abnormal.

## Women's Body, its Fragmentation and Psychological Repercussions

Fragmented body of women in general results into various psychological repercussions. The overwhelming concern in Morrison's novels is the African American women in particular and their bodies which are violated and abused. Women in her novels are always shown as victims of the system of race, slavery, and patriarchy. They have to go through severe physical pain and the intense traumatic experiences throughout their lives. They get experimented, beaten, whipped, sexually exploited or raped, and are left helpless in front of the White patriarch. Physical violence often entails inflicting physical, emotional, sexual and intellectual/psychological damage on the characters.

In *Beloved*, the female characters in the world they live i.e., of slavery, undergo victimization as a consequent of which they are fragmented of both the body as well as mind. Under slavery, as Morrison writes 'anyone white could take your whole self for anything that comes to mind' (Morrison 251) and can deny autonomy as well as render the self unrecognisable. As such, physically and mentally fragmented females in the novel, feel disconnected from themselves as well as from the community. Sethe cuts herself with an intent to suppress her traumatic past which is characterized by the psychological repercussions of rape and abuse.

The disintegration also renders the characters unable to see or recognize their own bodies. After Paul D's return Sethe recalls and reports him about her rape by the two White boys as the most painful physical fragmentation that she had undergone. She narrates the scene—two boys with mossy teeth, one sucking on her breast the other holding her down, their book-reading teacher watching and writing. She was so full of the disgusting memory that she was unable to go further back or recall it (Morison 83). Sethe even adds that her being off her husband not able to do anything implies her emotional fragmentation, that is, being away from the person with whom she is most close emotionally as well as physically. Halle was humiliated at witnessing the victimization of his wife.

In *The Second Sex* Simone de Beauvoir explicates the situation in which women are unable to protect their own bodies. Women recognize that the world is masculine on the whole; those who fashioned it, ruled it, and still dominate it today are men. As for her, she does not consider herself responsible for it; it is understood that she is inferior and dependent; she has not learned the lessons of violence, she has never stood forth as subject before the other members of the group. Shut up in her flesh, her home, she sees herself as passive before these gods with human faces who set goals and establish values.

The lot of women is respectful obedience. She has no grasp, even in thought, on the reality around her. It is opaque to her eyes (609). Evidently, Cee in *Home* had no idea about her own body being bruised in an experiment. She, under an intoxication of the drug injected by the doctor had to submit her body for his scientific or racial experiment. She did not know exactly what had been done to her body with the help of the sedatives. Her being naively deified the doctor but it was misused; her being and body were made to split, fragmented. Besides, Sethe in *Beloved* was obliged to submit her body to the White boys. It deems that had she learned the lesson of violence, she might have been able to defend herself. In this sense, violence also becomes a mode of defense or counter attack which she later exerts upon Beloved.

It is for the same reason, Sethe becomes so cruel that she strangles her own daughter Beloved out of her love and revenge to the brutal history (Morrison 175). A mother kills her child 'from love not hatred' (Ali 1420). The ghost of the murdered daughter makes her life more miserable to whom Sethe afterwards realizes that children are an integral part of herself. Beloved was the part forcefully splintered from her 'self' by slavery and patriarchy.

In *Beloved*, other female characters also suffer for psychologically repressing their traumatic past. Killing her daughter was a very detestable measure to take, but owing to the numbness inflicted upon her by her past, she loses her ability to think of any other way out. Also, it was the acting out of her own trauma inflicted upon her by slavery. Such violent acts according to Changizi and Ghasemi are 'a direct result of the traumatic experiences' (3) of abused women.

Morrison's depiction of rape and abuse in *Beloved* and *Home* accurately portrays the damaging effect that slavery had on those who were forced to carry its burden. Sethe suffers from the past which tends to torture her throughout her life. Likewise, for Cee too the damage done was lifelong, she cannot become a mother. Dr Beauregard's inhuman practice of putting her under an experiment renders Cee infertile. She is painfully haunted by incessant visions of a child. Besides, she is obsessed by the children smiling at her as if she were their mother: 'it's like there's a baby girl down here waiting to be born. She's somewhere close by in the air, in this house, and she picked me to be born to. And now she has to find some other mother' (Morrison 131). These hallucinations are the fragments of her wishes as a woman juxtaposed with her realities wielded forcefully upon her by the White male. They are the expressions of her grief that her fecundity for becoming a mother has been snatched away ruthlessly.

Fragmentation is most strongly suggested through *Beloved* at different levels: physical, mental and even historical. In her book *The Fragmented Female Body and Identity* B. June Pamela argues that fragmentation indicates the state of women's bodies, identities, memories, and relationships in the patriarchal era. Fragmentation contributes to a feminized lack of wholeness, and it is often symbolised fictively as bodily fragmentations, or physical wounds, scars and mutilations (4). As discussed by Pamela, the scar of the chokecherry on Sethe's back takes us back to a traumatic past that connotes a historical fragmentation. It was a testimony of the physical violence inflicted upon Sethe. As a slave woman, her body is dehumanized. Amy notices the image of a tree on Sethe's back because of the male physical brutality. It is not only the physical torn apart of Sethe's body, the split is emphasized even in the tree by spelling out all its divided parts i.e., its split trunk, the branches, and leaves.

> The chokecherry tree's trunk which is red and split wide open, full of sap, its parting for the branches, mighty lot of branches, the whole tree on her back is made out of the bruises of the lash while she got some whippings, divulge that the slaves were treated below the animals. A Mr Buddy had whipped her for her looking at him straight. (Morrison 93)

All these acts of brutality suggest a kind of meta-fragmentation because the image i.e., the tree, in relation to which Sethe's bodily fragmentation is described, itself is more subtly fragmented into the blooms, branches, leaves, trunk, etc. Besides, the symbol of the tree has spatial-temporal dimensions, connecting outward and the inward parts in space, and history and future in time (5). The obstacles confronting the characters while living in the world of slavery ensure fragmentation of both the body and mind. As it comes to mental fragmentation, Black women are the worst sufferers as they have been doubly oppressed because of their race and gender. Their suffering is not only physical, it exerts a life-long traumatic effect.

Sethe and Beloved act more cruelly in the novel. As Sheby Larrick in his chapter "Psychological Criticism of Tony Morrison's *Beloved* asserts that the severity of a character's actions are built on the psychological repression of their pasts (1). These pasts are filled with the trauma of slavery and sexual abuse. The past misery is teased out through the re-memory by which the female characters are haunted. The brutal violation of Sethe's body indicates her "mortification and diminishment" (Henderson 86) to a less than human status.

The school teacher on the basis of his privileged racial position divides Sethe in terms of her biological being sarcastically assessing her human and animalistic characteristics. He asks one of the men to put her human characteristics on the left, her animal ones on the right and to not forget to line them up (Morrison 228).

Doubly abused female bodies in the novel undergo severe pain throughout the novel. 'Whipping, lynching, rape, starvation, difficult labour, and physical torture are everyday practices' (Changizi and Ghasemi 1), the White patriarchs would exercise over the Black women's bodies. And the subjugation of female body leads to the subjugation of female self.

Thus, 'the disintegration of self is so complete in *Beloved* that the characters can't see or recognize their own bodies just as they are unable to tell their whole stories' (Powell 106). The physical torture, and labour and the humiliation that each slave, especially women endure 'leave them with nothing but a ruined body like Baby Suggs' or the damaged psyche like Sethe's which is epitomized in her infanticide and manner of rationalization' (Chagizi and Ghasemi 2).

In this way, Morrison's major characters are the fragmented individuals, disconnected from themselves, from each other as well as alienated from the community. Such alienation results in an emptiness that overpowers the individuals. Baby Suggs carries a sadness 'at her center, the dislocated center where the self that was no self, made its home' (106). Similarly, in *Home* Cee who has been depicted very naive, learns to recognize her body and her respectful being as time teaches her the lesson to count on herself. Miss Ethol strengthens Cee from within, "See what I mean? Look to yourself. You free ... don't let Lenore or some trifling boyfriend and certainly no devil doctor decide who you are. That's slavery" (Morrison 146).

For Morrison the ability to see one's self as physically whole and to appreciate the beauty of own's body is an integral part of knowing oneself. It is Baby Sugg's ultimate recognition of her own body that allows for salvation through the gathering together of her neighbors' bodies and stories in freedom.

Similarly, the racial fragmentation is evident in the depiction of the oppression of Negros by the Whites again leading to a suggestive bodily fragmentation, "Eighteen Seventy Four...

whole town wiped clean of Negros... grown men whipped like children; children whipped like adults; Black women raped by the crew; property taken, necks broken (213).

Sethe is not only the fragmented character in the novel, all the other female characters have also undergone equally tormenting split. For instance, Ella is locked up and repeatedly raped by a father and a son, whom she calls 'the lowest' (119) yet, and Stampaid's wife, Vashti, is forced into sex by her enslaver (184-232). Baby Suggs is compelled to have sex with her straw boss who later on breaks his coercive promise not to sell her child (23) and again with an overseer (144). Sethe's mother is taken up many times by the crew during the Middle Passage (62). Other allusions to sexual violation include the Sweet Home men's dreams of rape (10-11). The body is one site of operation for women and subjectivity is another.

However, Morrison seems not so pessimist in depicting only the predicament of women; rather she portrays her characters with some sense of rebellion, resistance and hope. The novel reveals how the condition of racial enslavement and patriarchal treachery in the external world, particularly the denial of one's status as human subject, had deep repercussions on the individual's internal worlds. These internal resonances are so profound that even if one is eventually freed from external bondage the self will still be trapped in an inner world that prevents a genuine experience of freedom. As Sethe exemplifies 'freeing oneself was one thing; claiming ownership of that freed self was another' (qtd. In Schapiro 1). In *Home* also Cee's physical freeing from the demon doctor is accomplished by Frank, her brother but it is suggested that freeing her inner self has yet to happen.

In *Home* and *Beloved*, Morrison not only depicts the pain and traumatic memory of physically and psychologically ruptured women but also writes about the need for them to form an integrated self in the face of a fragmented and unacceptable existence. Morrison implies that fiction provides the possibility of becoming coherent in a sexually hostile world. A method of narrating the past through which the fractures brought by enslavement and sexual treachery can be relived amidst the community, which might be soothing for the victims. Through the mode of sharing, Morrison indicates that the difficult task of fusing such fractures thereby initiates the possibility of coherence and recognition for the characters. In *Beloved* the women characters move through alliance with the community towards freedom. Through the recollection and retelling of fragmented life stories and by forming them into a coherent whole, the characters of *Beloved* free themselves, yoke together stories and bodies, spirit and flesh and begin forging a sense of self that holds promise for the future. They do the same in *Home* after bringing Cee to their community; they attend, cure, nurse and educate her to be strong and authentic.

Irrespective of the prejudices and their repercussions, the novels have an ending that promises hope. Throughout the troubling years of Sethe's life on her period of abjection, Denver was growing to be a young woman and she experiences her own subjectivity as a creative healing (Mayfield 10). Denver is helped by Mrs Bodwin and other community women including Sethe to get experiences, be educated and establish her independent selfhood. As Barnett suggests, 'sexual exploitation is not only the Black women's story of slavery'. As Sethe suggests in *Beloved*, women irrespective of their ages and races, come together against their plight (425).

*Beloved* suggests that it is through shared recognition and understanding of historical fragmentation that women can begin to heal one another. Morrison suggests that hope is available to us, that all women like young Denver at the end of *Beloved* can also be spared of sexual injustice if only female communities work together (135).

## Conclusion

Thus, Morrison's *Home* and *Beloved* revolve around the fragmentation of women characters who fail to see or recognize their bodies, feel splintered from their selves as well as disconnected from the community. All the female characters undergo emotional, sexual and psychological damage inflicted by the often intersecting agencies of oppression, patriarchy and racism. With Sethe, fragmentation affects at different levels: physical, mental and historical. Her self is fractured due to the demeaning experience of rape back at Sweet Home. She feels that the 'stealing of her milk' by the nephews of the schoolteacher has seized her authority over her own body. The dehumanizing whippings of her masters have left her back inscribed with an image of a tree, rendering it lifeless. The image of the tree on Sethe's back and the frequent sexual assault all the female characters experience foreground age-long history of women's fragmentation. Likewise, the medical experiment over Cee's womb is an invasion of her body. Her rescue by her brother and healing by the community women implies solidarity and sisterhood.

Physically and psychologically damaged women in the novels eventually begin to realize the need to rebel. At the same time, consolidation of women also becomes inevitable for retelling their painful history and asserting themselves. Communal integration and assistance prove to be effective instruments for healing of the ruptured being of women. How communal integration of Black women worked in healing the trauma inflicted upon them by slavery and patriarchy will be discussed in another chapter.

## Works Cited

Ali, Hira. "Gender Analysis in Toni Morrison's Beloved and Sula." *Middle-East Journal of Scientific Research*, vol. 16, no. 10, 2013, pp. 1419-1423.

Bartky, S. L. Feminity and Domination: Studies in the Phenomenology of Oppression. New York: Routledge, 1990.

— "Foucault, Feminity, and the Modernization of Patriarchal Power."

*Feminism and Foucault: Reflection of Resistance.* Eds. I. Diamond and L.Quinby. Boston: North Eastern University Press, 1988.

Beauvoir, Simone de. *The Second Sex.* UK: Vintage, 1997. Print.

Bloom, Sandara L. "Understanding the impact of sexual Assault: The Nature of Traumatic Experience." *Sexual Assault: Victimization Across the Lifespan.* Ed. Giardino, A. and et al. Missouri: Medical Publishing, 2003, pp. 405-432.

Butler, Judith. *Bodies that Matter.* New York: Routledge, 1993.

Changizi, Parisa and Parvin Ghasemi. "A Focauldian Reading of Tony Morrison's *Beloved.*" *Journal of Research in Peace, Gender and Development*, vol 2, Jan 2012, pp. 1-5.

Fredrickson, Barbara L. and Tomi-Ann Roberts. "Objectification Theory: Towards Understanding Women's lived Experiences and Mental Health Risks." *Psychology of Women Quarterly*, vol. 21, 1997, pp. 137-206.

Henderson, M. G. "Toni Morrison's *Beloved*: Re-Membering the Body as Historical Text." *Toni Morrison's Beloved.* Eds. Andrews and Mc Kay. 79-106.

Hooks, bell. *Feminism is for Everybody: Passionate Politics.*

South End Press, 1984.

King, Angela. "The Prisoner of Gender: Foucault and the Disciplining of the Female Body." *The Journal of Women's Studies.* vol. 5, no. 2, 2004.

Larrick, Shelby. "Psychological Criticism of Tony Morrison's Beloved." *A Web Case Book on Beloved by Toni Morrison.* 2007.

Morrison, Toni. *Beloved.* Knopf, 1987.

—. *Home.* Chato & Windos, 2012.

Pamela B. June. *The Fragmented Female Body and Identity.* Peter Lang Publishing, 2010.

Powell, Betty Jane. "'Will the parts hold?': The Journey Towards a Coherent Self in *Beloved.*" *Colby Quarterly*, vol. 31, no. 2, 1995, pp. 105-113.

Schapiro, Barbara. "The Bond of Love and the Boundaries of Self in Toni Morrison's *Beloved.*" *Contemporary Literature* XXXII, 1991.

CHAPTER 5

# *Playing in the Dark* and the American Fairy Tale

Tamara Miles

FAIRY TALES often depend on transformation from weak to strong, from vulnerable to victorious, from invisible to visible. This seems to be part of Toni Morrison's message in her pivotal nonfiction work *Playing in the Dark*, in which she explores the structure of society built on whiteness as the comparative norm, and how that norm is reflected in the national literature of that place. People of color became invisible to Whites as explored in Ralph Ellison's *Invisible Man* because Whites are blinded by their own worldview, caught in a cultural mindset that is not easy to escape. It takes a shift from willful ignorance to conscious examination of the self and the other. In this essay, I examine *Playing in the Dark* as a lens that can help people approach a more authentic human experience that rises above play-acting and fairy tales.

Recently, I painted a scene from Little Red Riding Hood. My heroine in her flaming red, beautiful robe and hood appeared to be an adult, ghostly pale... In short, she looked like me. She had a deeply troubled version of my own face. The woods surrounding her were predictably dark and deep, but what was I doing in this fairy tale, and why had I painted myself so glaringly white? As the author of *Picturing the Rose: A Way of Looking at Fairy Tales* has explained, women in fairy tales are often doing something forbidden… going on a quest, away from their father's protection, for example. Other women are 'depicted as possessing great powers, either through the choices they make or through the use of supernatural or spiritual forces. Women can affect events because of their appetites, sexual or other' (30-31). This dichotomy splits the self into victim or victor, and neither classification fully represents the female spirit. A similar risk occurs when White writers attempt to portray Black characters and their experiences because White writers are writing about an unknown aspect of the human experience. Despite their best intentions, they cannot fully represent the Black experiences even in fiction, when imagination is given full play.

Vladimir Nabokov claimed that novels are above all fairy tales. His *Lolita* embodies 'the themes of deception, enchantment, and metamorphosis' (Appel qtd. in Jones) that we often see in fairy tales. He 'seems to suggest … that man lives between two worlds, the imagined one and the 'true' one … and that art—folk and literary—is a conscious exploitation of this situation' (Jones). As Morrison explains, writers want to make their readers familiar with what is unfamiliar, and 'mystify the familiar' to give it greater power and meaning. But 'a teller can only reflect what she knows or what she can hypothesize, imagine, or foresee' (Lane 30). This is why Morrison reminds us to consider the one who writes as much as what is written. Recently, I complained to my daughter about the ignorance of certain political perspectives, to which she responded, 'Yes, but that is what they know.' This is the truth of the world as they understand it. Similarly, when a story is written, it becomes a permanent record of someone's truth at the time of the writing. It cannot be taken back. It has become a real thing (Lane 44).

That truth, for White writers portraying Black characters, is limited and shaped by the white world view. Throughout history, Whites have deceived themselves in one way or another about the Black experience (this ranges from profoundly seeing the African Americans as less human, ordained by God to be slaves, inferior spiritually and intellectually, sexually irresponsible, and so forth to the extreme opposite of claiming there is no difference at all, color doesn't matter, white privilege/racism no longer exists among the majority, etc.) Clearly, we are still divided in significant ways, haunted by our past. The present is still clouded with confusion, suspicion, guilt, blame, anger, and other overwhelming emotions.

In "Finding the Other: The Radical Vision of Toni Morrison," Jesse McCarthy recalls 'the brutal shadow of slavery still darkening the horizon.' She says, 'It captures the spectrum of light from the horizon, where surface and sky seem to meet, to the deepest shadows below the surface.' But this definition of horizon accompanies another—the limitations of a person's perspective according to experience and interest. McCarthy observes in the writings of Virginia Woolf and others the long-held association of Black people with labour, toiling in the sun and swamp, exploited. She points to the social criticism at the heart of Woolf's approach, which stirs the 'layers of consciousness that operate just below our cultivated personalities.' Too often, we avoid the hidden other by denying, repressing, refusing to see, and this is a collective problem that must be addressed collectively. Instead, our national literature has often simply omitted the subject and 'pretended not to be concerned with race' (McCarthy). Morrison, however, has dug in the literary dirt and revealed the unattended bones. She is a 'moral anthropologist' whose specialties are the living tombs of the novel and essay (McCarthy).

Ideally, when we read, we meet the other in memory and in context, and our horizon expands. The dispossessed bones rise and take shape. They walk among us again and breathe their stories, and we find our common humanity if we are willing to listen and speak to them. Morrison walks with us as a translator, and for those of us who are bankrupt of feelings, she coaxes us towards renewal and compassion. She bids us to come out of our bunkers and silos and consider whether we are a human community who must together face our greatest threats (McCarthy). We are the big bad wolves and the little red riding hoods making our way through the racial forest.

In a fairy tale, it is clear who is the trickster and who is the vulnerable wayfarer. We have learned that the trickster will be exposed and all will be well. In real life, this may still be our position: someone else is the problem, the evil stranger who cannot be trusted, and we are the innocents. Our treatment of the other in this way involves two tools described by Morrison: metaphysical condensation and fetishization (67). Through condensation, we attempt to 'transform social and historical differences into universal differences ... persons into animals,' preventing meaningful communication (67). Through fetishization, we evoke fears and desires by emphasizing differences when little or no difference exists (for example, in blood—characterizing black or white blood, good blood, bad blood, and so forth). We try to 'assert the categorical absolutism of civilization and savagery' (67). Who is the savage?

That wolves are demonized is a problem to be addressed more fully in another essay, but suffice it to say that African American men have been and are equally demonized in literature and society. In regard to the famous novel *Heart of Darkness*, by Joseph Conrad, Chinua Achebe has observed how the author's African characters lack full humanity and expression, and how the darkness of Black people and even the whole African continent is emphasized and 'portrayed as uncivilized and set in contrast to European civilization' (qtd. in McParland). As for the fragile, vulnerable White woman so often portrayed by the African American women are perhaps the most vulnerable population on the planet. They are also perhaps the most determined to be powerful and free. We make a mistake to underestimate the reassembly of their collective bones and their confrontation with oppressors. What a distressing surprise and revelation it can be for the White society to see the savage, the wolf, in the mirror!

What of the hunter, the one who cuts open the wolf's stomach, frees Little Red Riding Hood and her grandmother, and then celebrates with them? 'The hunter or huntsman is a traditional figure in folklore... One quality generally associated with these hunters is their skill with guns or bows and arrows. The phallic connotations of these chapters suggest that hunters possess the knowledge and ability to achieve sexual congress, and that, in a sense, what they are hunting for (their prey) is a sexual partner' (Jones). Mark Whalan has examined Sherwood Anderson's fascination with American Black men and asked, 'Why are his descriptions of watching African

American laborers—often from concealed positions {*like a hunter*?}—so infused with anxiety, envy, and celebration?' This reference to the author's hiding while he watches seems central to White authors who try to write about Black people. Regarding Anderson, Whalan suggests, 'African American men in particular seemed to him to be engaged in older, more communal, and craft-based models of working practice and have a virility and sexual dominance missing from the White working-class men.' Over time, he seems to have developed a better understanding of the 'commodification of race' that reshaped his more primitivist ideas (Whalan). As Whalan further acknowledges, this preoccupation with primitivism carried great cultural weight in America not only in literature but in other fields. Anthropology was not the only discipline of the time using 'the primitive' for purposes of cultural criticism: psychology, with its interest in the violent, selfish, and sexual desires of the unconscious, saw an anthropological analogue in supposedly 'savage peoples' (Whalan). As for Anderson, Whalan argues, African Americans were central to (his) perception of the South, of sexuality, and of American economics for the majority of his writing career. And he is hardly the only one to hypersexualize and hyper-racialize. We are creatures of extremes, and these extremes are evident in our literature.

Paccaud-Huguet and Abouddahab have referred to fiction as 'the privileged framework, the other scene in space and time ('not here, not now') providing the perfect alibi—literally, an elsewhere—for facing, framing, and containing the other's desire and the strange libido attached to violence.' Furthermore, fairy tale characters such as the wolf or the Little Red Riding

Hood are 'shifting positions: they are *not me,* thus I am allowed to participate in a way that does not eclipse the "real me" with which I identify' (Paccaud-Huguet and Abouddahab). I can remain pure. However, some authors and artists have responded to fairy tales with their own anti-tales that challenge the separateness. In Tomoko Konoike's illustrations of Little Red Riding Hood, 'the wolf, who is supposed to be the heroine's aggressor, is multiplied and constitutes the upper part of her own body' (Calvin and McAra). This reimagining is the kind of work Morrison seems to be exploring in *Playing in the Dark.*

We must go beyond what Zoe Wicomb calls the 'benign concession' to race, beyond marginalization and subjectivity when we narrate the human story, which is part fable given the short span of our memory. The paradigm of black and white needs critical focus and resistance on the part of both groups (Wicomb qtd in Phiri). Wicomb's novel *Playing in the Light* is a 'homage' to Morrison, she explains in an interview with Aretha Phiri. It speaks of 'playing white' as well as to the advantages of lightness (qtd in Phiri). In South Africa, the author explains, 'Such crossing over by coloured people was of course shrouded in secrecy. Many coloured people of a certain age know of neighbours or family members who disappeared, faded overnight into whiteness, but that is all we knew' (qtd in Phiri).

This reference brings to mind the story of Snow White and the three drops of blood that fall into snow that has piled up on a black windowsill at the beginning, when the Queen pricks her finger. She wishes for a daughter whose skin is white as snow, with raven hair, and red lips, and that wish is granted. All is well until the queen dies and the wicked stepmother becomes envious of Snow White's beauty because she is 'fairer'—the 'fairest' of them all. Envy and jealousy are, in part, a fear of disappearing, being replaced and forgotten. In *The Bluest Eye*, in which a Black girl dreams of having blue eyes, Morrison herself 'weaves a fable about the relationship between conformity and experiment, survival and creativity' (Christian).

When the Queen orders the Huntsman to take Snow White into the woods, kill her, and bring her heart back as proof, our heroine cries, 'Spare me this mockery of justice! I will run away into the forest and never come home again!' Of the people who 'played white' in South Africa for a better life, Wicomb writes, 'Their new lives, circumscribed by a number of laws, all ensured that there would be no social contact with their families. Now in political terms you may have contempt for play-whites; but as a writer I am interested in what it means for individuals born into a society that is hyper-religious and committed to family values to renounce their families' (qtd in Phiri). I imagine this painful situation as like Snow White buried in the glass casket with a piece of poisoned apple stuck in her throat. Toni Morrison's *Playing in the Dark* is a means of dislodging that poisoned apple. Her own fiction can be like a folktale:

> As the author, she is beyond time, collapsing the past, present, and future into the now so we might understand and feel the significance… It is as if we were hearing an old African folktale—mythological in tone—in which content revitalizes an empty terminological system. The then is in the now; the now in the then; and the teller spins ever-intricate webs of connectiveness, until the web is completed or broken. (Jones)

Fairy tales contain both threat and reassurance (*San Francisco Chronicle*, qtd. in Morrison). 'What we imagine, we become', claims Morrison (3). We 'contemplate chaos and civilization' (Morrison 7) when we enter the dark woods of fairy tales. We also tell ourselves about the African American experience.

Let us consider again the Trickster, a character that appears in many folktales and myths from around the world. As Lane observes, a Trickster may be employed in the tale as a fool, a clown, or a powerful creative force (45) depending on the culture from which the story arises. Those who revere the Trickster as an important part of the spiritual world may find the reduction of this character disappointing, troubling, and offensive. This idea is one that crosses over into Morrison's critical examination of the Black people as characters in the White imagination. She admits that as a reader, she first believed that Black people as treated by White writers did not signify much beyond local color, pathos, or humor (14). When she began to read like a writer, she saw the self-consciousness that lay across the pages when White writers wrote about Black people, about the other (15). It is presented in signs, codes, and strategies. The treatment of Black subjects may appear decorative or illusory, but it is also reflexive and revelatory of the white consciousness that fashions it, of its longings and its terror (16). When Morrison describes Willa Cather's novel *Sapphira and the Slave Girl* as itself a fugitive among Cather's works, she implies it is a thing (a body?) that got lost from the writer's consciousness. That consciousness works to hide from itself as surely as the enslaved character is forced to hide her thoughts, emotions, and even her body for the sake of her own safety (20).

Hiding and distraction are central to many fairy tales. Lane recounts the tale of travelers who must spend the night in the forest, all the while fearing the wild beasts. They spend the night alternately keeping watch. In their effort to distract themselves while each takes his duty, one carves a doll, one designs a dress to clothe the doll, and the third prays the doll into human existence. Then they begin to argue over who owns the doll … to whom does she belong? 'I carved her', the first says. 'I dressed her', responds the second. 'I gave her life', claims the third (66). To resolve the matter, they ask a witness to decide. We might say that the writer does each of these, but is surprised when the doll he has invented takes on a life of its own before the witness reader and begins to ask questions. Morrison points out that *Sapphira and the Slave Girl* is Cather's 'dreaming and re-dreaming her problematic relationship with her own mother' (26); it is about self as much as about the other.

Finally, in fairy tales, the possibility of miracles exists. What a miracle it would be if White consciousness expanded to a greater capacity for understanding in its treatment of human consciousness that includes Black subjects. Morrison refers to 'the shadow that is companion to this whiteness' (33) as if it travels along in the woods of consciousness as a player in the great fairy tale still unfolding, in which we all hope for miracles but continue walking our path towards some mysterious place, following the secret map of Morrison's *Playing in the Dark.*

## Works Cited

Calvin, David, and Catriona McAra. *Anti-Tales: The Uses of Disenchantment.* Cambridge Scholars Publishing, 2011.

Christian, Barbara. "The Contemporary Fables of Toni Morrison." *Sula – Toni Morrison*, Chelsea House, 2021. *Bloom's Literature*, online.infobase.com/Auth/Index?aid=101297&itemid=WE54&articleId=477038. Accessed 13 June 2021.

Jones, Steven Swann. "Folk Characterization in *Lolita*." *Lolita, Original Edition*, Chelsea House, 1992. *Bloom's Literature*, online.infobase.com/Auth/Index?aid=101297&itemid=WE54&articleId=623208. Accessed 16 June 2021.

Lane, Marcia. *Picturing the Rose: A Way of Looking at Fairy Tales.* H.W. Wilson, 1994.

McCarthy, Jesse. "Finding the Other." *Nation*, vol. 309, no. 16, Dec. 2019, pp. 27-32. *EBSCOhost*, search.ebscohost.com/login.aspx?direct=true&db=aph&AN=140306681&site=ehost-live.

Morrison, Toni. Playing *in the Dark: Whiteness and the Literary Imagination*. Vintage Books, 1993.

Paccaud-Huguet, Josiane, and Rédouane Abouddahab. *Fiction, Crime, and the Feminine.* Cambridge Scholars Publishing, 2011.

Phiri, Aretha. "Black, White and Everything in-between:

Unravelling the Times with Zoe Wicomb." *English in Africa*, vol. 45, no. 2, August 2018, pp. 117-128. EBSCOhost, doi:10.4314/eia.v45i2.9.

Silver, Andrew. "Making Minstrelsy of Murder: George Washington Harris, The Ku Klux Klan, and the Reconstruction Aesthetic of Fright." *Nineteenth-Century Literature Criticism*, edited by Kathy D. Darrow, vol. 232, 2011. Gale Literature Resource Center, Link.gale.com/apps/doc/H1420102403/GLS?u=orgtec&sid+bookmark-GLS&&xid=99763043. Accessed 16 June 2021. Originally published in *Minstrelsy and Murder: The Crisis of Southern Humor, 1835-1925*. Louisiana State University Press, 2006, pp. 49-87.

Whalan, Mark. "Sherwood Anderson and Primitivism." *Short Story Criticism*, edited by Catherine C. DiMercurio, vol. 270, Gale, 2019. *Gale Literature Resource Center*, link.gale.com/apps/doc/H1420126433/GLS?u=orgtec&sid=bookmark-GLS&xid=bef745c1. Accessed 16 June 2021. Originally published in *Race, Manhood, and Modernism in America*, U of Tennessee P, 2007, pp. 73-122.

CHAPTER 6

# Of Unspeaking Mothers and Unforgiving Daughters

## The Trauma of Broken Mother-Child Relation in *A Mercy*

Saikat Sarkar

MOTHERHOOD IS a central and recurring theme in Morrison's novels and she also invests in this subject frequently in her essays, lectures and interviews. Motherhood, a traditional space of security, is revised and scrutinized by Morrison to contextualize her narratives against the oppressive socio-cultural contexts against which the African Americans had to survive in America for centuries. From her first novel *The Bluest Eye* (1970) to her last, *God Help the Child* (2015) Morrison has delved deep into the psychological scar and trauma generated by the troubled mother-child relationship. In her ninth novel *A Mercy* (2008) Morrison again engages with the vulnerability of mother-daughter relationship to underscore the humanity of Black mothers forced to operate within inhuman pressure exercised by slavery.

*A Mercy* can be read as a prequel to Morrison's most famous novel *Beloved* (1987). If in *Beloved* Sethe attempts to kill all her four children, while managing to cut one to death, in order to save them from being dragged into a lifetime of slavery by the slave owners, in *A Mercy* also, one sees a slave mother giving up her young daughter Florens to serve a man who appears to her eyes as a kind-hearted man and hence a better alternative than her current employer. Set in colonial America *A Mercy* is an exploration of a broken mother-daughter relationship which results in psychic rupture and imparity of communication. In this paper I would attempt to examine how in her novels in general and *A Mercy* in particular, Morrison builds upon and re-inscribes on the difficult experiences of Black women as mothers to form a different perspective of motherhood. Additionally, this paper would also explore how Morrison constructs a distinctive view of Black motherhood in her novel which demands to be approached and understood as radically different from the image of motherhood ingrained in and endorsed by the dominant White American culture.

On July 15, 2005 during a public interview held in Cincinnati Music Hall named "On Stage with Toni Morrison and Richard Danielpour" Morrison declared that she was planning to write two more novels. This happened the night after Danielpour's opera *Margaret Garner: A New American Opera* premiered in Cincinnati, Ohio. Morrison was the librettist of that opera. The reason behind using this bit of information at the beginning of this essay is manifold. The story of Margaret Garner has had a huge impact on Morrison and this directly resulted in her most celebrated novel *Beloved* (1987). Sethe's apparently horrific and un-understandable act of trying to kill her children is premised upon the life of the female slave Margaret Garner who in reality did the same thing. Morrison came across the life of Garner and this striking incident while rummaging through sundry materials for *The Black Book* (1974), a collage-like scrapbook encasing the history and experience of the African Americans in the US which

Morrison was editing for Random House. In a conversation with the novelist Gloria Naylor Morrison talks about how she got the idea of writing *Beloved* from the life of Garner:

> ...I do remember being obsessed by two or three little fragments of stories that I heard from different places. One was a newspaper clipping about a woman named Margaret Garner in 1851. ...she had escaped from Kentucky ... with her four children. She succeeded in killing one; she tried to kill two others. She hit them in the head with a shovel and they were wounded but they didn't die. And there was a smaller one that she had at her breast. The interesting thing, in addition to that, was the interviews that she gave. She was a young woman. In the inked pictures of her she seemed a very quiet, very serene-looking woman and everyone who interviewed her remarked about her serenity and tranquillity. She said, 'I will not let those children live where I lived.' (Naylor 206-07)

In another interview with Bill Moyers Morrison observes;

> Her mother-in-law, who was a preacher, said, 'I watched her do it. And I neither encouraged her nor discouraged her.' So, for them, it was a dilemma. Shall I permit my children, who are my best thing, to live like I have lived, when I know that's terrible? So, she decided to kill them and kill herself. That was noble. (Moyers 272)

This is remarkable poise in the face of adversity and cannot be negated as insanity which is a stereotypical way of White America to describe the African American.

Moreover, the state in which this opera premiered also played a significant role during the time of slavery as well as in Morrison's fictions. In an interview with Robert Stepto in 1976 Morrison describes the state:

> Ohio is right on the Kentucky border, so there's not much difference between it and the "South". It's an interesting state from the point of view of Black people because it is right there by the Ohio River, in the South and at its Northern tip is Canada. And there were these fantastic abolitionists there, and also the Ku Klux Klan lived there. (Stepto 12)

In another interview with Claudia Tate (1983) Morrison further emphasizes this dual nature of the state of Ohio which houses conflicted and contradictory approaches to life:

> The Northern part of the state had underground railroad stations and a history of Black people escaping into Canada, but the Southern part of the state is as much Kentucky as there is, complete with cross burnings. Ohio is a curious juxtaposition of what was ideal in this country and what was base. It was also a Mecca for Black people; they came to the mills and plants because Ohio offered the possibility of a good life, the possibility of freedom, even though there were some terrible obstacles. Ohio also offered an escape from stereotyped Black settings. It is neither plantation nor ghetto. (Tate 158)

This in-between nature of the state of Ohio is emblematic of the unstable conditions that African American in America have faced for centuries.

And finally, of the two novels planned *A Mercy* (2008) was to be the first one[1]. *A Mercy* thematically revisits the unspeakable and undecipherable motherly act of Margaret Garner from the history of United Sates and Sethe from the world of fiction. One significant aspect of *A Mercy* is that apart from *Beloved* which is set in mid nineteenth century all the other novels barring *A Mercy* are set in the backdrop of contemporary America. With *A Mercy* Morrison decides to go even further back than the time of *Beloved* and chooses the late seventeenth century as the setting of the novel. This is because in this novel Morrison "wanted to separate race from slavery to see what it was like, what it might have been like, to be a slave but without being raced; where your status was being enslaved but there was no application of racial inferiority" (radio interview with Lynn Neary). The novel bears witness to the historical-cultural reality that the interweaving of slavery and racism was not born naturally but has resulted from a traceable concerted effort in which different institutions played a part. *A Mercy* is located in the Virginia colony of 1690 when the nature of America had fluidity and the racial divide was not rigid. This was also the time when White men of European descent were employed as slaves. But this was on the verge of changing and the institution of slavery in different states was gradually getting racialized.

*A Mercy* talks back to various other novels of Morrison. As has been mentioned earlier the theme motherhood and the disturbed mother-child bond is a recurrent theme in Morrison's fictional oeuvre and from her very first novel, *The Bluest Eye* it has played a significant role in weaving her worldview as expressed through her novels. Technically too, *A Mercy* shares with its predecessors Morrison's favoured practice of setting up her narrative through different points of view[2]. The point of view from that of Florens, a part-African, part-European teenaged girl who narrates her story through first person and a nameless third person narrator who provides us with the back stories. In the final chapter, Morrison introduces the point of view of Florens' mother misunderstood by Florens through her life for what she thought to be an act of selfishness. Only in the end the reader comes to know the true reason behind her act and realizes that it was an act of motherly sacrifice.

The novel relates the story of Jacob Vaark, who has come to America from Europe as a distantly related uncle leaves him 200 acres of land in the new nation and settles down to run a farm with the help of Rebekka, his young wife who comes from England, and three Black women – Lina, their native American servant whom they take in as an orphan, Sorrow, the daughter of a sea-captain and an unskilled one and Florens, whom Vaark brings from a farm run by Senor D'Ortega to relieve Rebekka of the pain of having lost her first born Patrician. The novel also rings with references of a rebellion which was enraged in Virginia in 1675 and was led by Nathaniel Bacon. Known as the 'people's war', this rebellion is alluded to by the narrator, "Half a dozen years ago an army of Blacks, Natives, Whites, Mulattoes—freedmen, slaves and indentured—had waged war against local gentry led by the members of the very class" (*A Mercy* 8). The rebellion was thwarted but this set the premise for the novel which unfolds against a backdrop of civil unrest, a time when persecution in the name of religion was quite common as colonies in New England labelled themselves 'Bible Commonwealths' and tried to follow the dictates of the Bible verbatim. This was a time when slavery was still not based on the colour of one's skin. Even the Europeans were enslaved. Vaark's farm itself has two European slaves, Willard and Scully.

*A Mercy* re-works the central theme of *Beloved*—a mother sacrificing her child to save her (a daughter in both the cases) from a life of drudgery. But unlike Sethe in *Beloved* who murdered her daughter, the unnamed mother of Florens in *A Mercy* gives up her daughter to a slave-owner in the hope of providing her with a better life than hers. Nevertheless, the act is a momentous one as it revises the traditional concept of motherhood with biting and yet touching irony. According to the conventional notions, a mother is supposed to be the safest harbour for a child, a shelter from danger. Florens is given up by her mother, which is prompted by a pathetic and desperate hope for procuring a better life for the child. Florens's mother took a major risk as she calculated that Jacob Vaark would be a better and kinder slave-master than the one she herself had been serving under. In the last part of the novel the reader realizes the true intention of the mother as she speaks out:

> One chance, I thought. There is no protection but there is difference. You stood there in those shoes and the tall man laughed and said he would take me to close the debt. I knew Senhor would not allow it. I said you. Take you, my daughter. Because I saw the tall man see you as a human child, not pieces of eight. I knelt before him. Hoping for a miracle. He said yes.
>
> It was not a miracle. Bestowed by God. It was a mercy. Offered by a human. (*A Mercy 164-65*)

She is not named in the novel and is mentioned as minha mãe which in Portuguese means 'my mother'. This is in commensuration with the Portuguese owner of the farm she was a slave in. This owner D'Ortega has fallen under debt of Jacob Vaark and as a repayment offered one of his slaves. Though initially reluctant, Jacob finally relents and decides on Florens' mother but D'Ortega refuses to give her up on the pretext of her being important to his wife. It becomes apparent that he himself was exploiting her sexually. Florens' mother saw that her master's interest was gradually shifting to Florens and as an act of motherly protection, a protection which belies the understanding of traditional motherly role.

The novel is contextualized against the backdrop of America in the last part of the $17^{th}$ century, when legal discrimination against the African Americans was still in the process of being formed. Morrison writes about a people's rebellion that happened in the 1670s which included both the African Americans and the Whites fighting together. But things changed when this rebellion was thwarted and new laws were framed:

> By eliminating manumission, gatherings, travel and bearing arms for Black people only; by granting license to any White to kill any Black for any reason; by compensating owners for a slave's maiming or death, they separated and protected all Whites from all others forever. Any social ease between gentry and laborers, forged before and during that rebellion, crumbled beneath a hammer and wielded in the interests of the gentry's profits. (*A Mercy 8*)

In this context, when the menace of slavery was exerting its stronghold over the African Americans, the anonymous mother sacrificed her daughter by giving her away to a slave-owner who she hoped would be kind to her child. Though Florens moved from the cruelties of Ortega's plantation to the relative ease of Jacob Vaark's farm, the pain involved in the mother's action does not escape the reader. Through this individual action and a comparable action of Sethe that took place hundred years later, Morrison encapsulates a painful truth about slavery; that of enforced sacrifices and disintegrating families.

In her study *Toni Morrison and Motherhood: A Politics of the Heart*, Andrea O'Reilly observes how in her novels Morrison goes on to resist the racist stereotyping of slave mothers. Homi Bhabha has shown how racist stereotyping has had a major role in the discursive domination of the colonized subjects by the colonizers.[3] O'Reilly cites Patricia Hill Collins to contend that in American imagination "the four controlling images" of African American mother "include the mammy, the matriarch, the welfare mother, and the Jezebel" (2). Collins in *Black Feminist Thought: Knowledge, Consciousness, and the Politics of Empowerment* contends that the Black women:

> fashioned an independent standpoint about the meaning of Black womanhood. These self-definitions enabled Black women to use African derived conceptions of self and community to resist negative evaluations of Black womanhood advanced by dominant groups. In all, Black women's grounding in traditional African American culture fostered the development of a distinctive African American women's culture. (11)

African American literature and especially women's

literature has been a conscious effort to resist such stereotypical representations. Audre Lorde argues, "[I]t is axiomatic that if we do not define ourselves for ourselves, we will be defined by others—for their use and to our detriment" (cited by Collins 21). This attempt at self-definition is what gets reflected in *A Mercy* as well as in many other novels of Morrison.

O'Reilly opines that the African American act of motherhood is aimed at psychological healing and the empowerment of children. Life under slavery is bound to leave scars for the African American children and also leave them traumatized. The task of the mother is to address and counter this and as a result, African American motherhood has to be seen as a politico-cultural act. For O'Reilly African American motherhood can be understood through five interrelated concepts; "'Othermothering and Community Mothering,' 'Motherhood as Social Activism and as a Site of Power,' 'Matrifocality,' 'Nurturance as Resistance: Providing a Homeplace,' and 'The Motherline: Mothers as Cultural Bearers'" (4). She goes on to elaborate these as offering protection to the children which even the biological mother cannot do or to instil in the children a sense of inclusivity which, in turn, fosters a transformative power for them. The matrifocal Black community has mothers as its structural centre and hence, the easy binary divide of public and private sphere does not operate. This countering of the segregation on the basis of sex also enables the mother to transform the private sphere in a homeplace—a place where nurturance leads to resistance. This resistance to discursive formation begins at home for the African Americans under the tutelage of African American mothers. O'Reilly also holds African American mothers as traditional custodians of the community's culture and tradition.

Toni Morrison's fictional oeuvre is replete with instances of mothers in families that are reeling under the aftermath of slavery. Although, *Beloved* and *A Mercy* are situated in times much after the end of slavery, they bring forth the long term impact of the detrimental effects of slavery and the resultant psychological disintegration. In these two novels the situation faced by the mothers are much harsher and the trauma is more severe. Bell hooks has aptly posited that "[i]n the midst of a brutal racist system, which did not value black life, [the slave mother] valued the life of her child enough to resist that system" (44). For the slave mother living under slavery the task of offering protection to her child needs immediate decisive action. Both the mothers in *Beloved* and *A Mercy* responded to immediate crises in a way that is difficult to grasp not only for us but also for their children for whom they made such sacrifices. In *Beloved* the slayed child comes back to haunt Sethe years later and in *A Mercy* Florens grows up misunderstanding her mother and harbouring a grudge against her.

Florens, who is seven or eight, remembers with sadness and grief the pain of being sent away by her mother;

> forever and ever. Me watching, my mother listening, her baby boy on her hip. Senhor is not paying the whole amount he owes to Sir. Sir saying he will take instead the woman and the girl, not the baby boy and the debt is gone. A minha mãe begs no. Her baby boy is still at her breast. Take the girl, she says, my daughter, she says. Me. Me (*A Mercy 7*)

She grows up having a negative reaction against mothers and babies in general and nurtures in her a hatred that takes away the quotient of love which she is capable of. What she does not realise is the real reason behind her mother's decision to let her go. Slavery as an institution had dehumanized so many people that it is difficult to keep count and only through such imaginative revisiting can we realize, even if partially, the depth of the trauma. The novel gradually unfolds its narrative and only in the end one comes to know the real reason. Meanwhile, Morrison takes us through a difficult time both in the lives of the women in the farm as well as in the history of the nation. Rebekka, called Mistress, has fallen ill. She is the wife of the now deceased Jacob Vaark, the owner of the farm. She was also brought from England to marry Jacob as her father was unable to incur the cost of bearing her. If this in a way reflects the story of Florens, Rebekka has been subjected through more pain because of losing her children at childbirth and also, losing one when her child was an infant. Messalina, a native American girl and Sorrow, a Black American are the other two women on the farm. The novel follows the journey of Florens who goes in search of an African blacksmith who once worked on Jacob's farm and had cured Sorrow of small pox. Later, however, Jacob dics from it and his wife gets affected with the same disease. *A Mercy* takes the reader along the late seventeenth century America as Florens finds the blacksmith and later falls in love with him. The question remains whether she will return or choose to remain a free woman.

In the end, she returns to the farm but the reader sees that on her way she behaves cruelly with a boy living under the care of the blacksmith. Such act of cruelty is a result of her broken self, broken under the pressure of thinking that her mother let her go because she did not love her. Morrison makes us realize that we would need a different parameter to gauge the acts of motherly love by the Black American mothers, one that is not sanctioned by the yardstick of mainstream culture. Florens' mother understood how D'Ortega was gradually shifting his attention to Florens and realized what it meant for the young girl. If she were chosen by Jacob Vaark, she would in all probability get a better life as Varrk seemed like a rare man who was not sexually objectifying her. But she knew that without her the infant son would die and also that it was Florens who deserved this chance of getting away from D'Ortega, this act of mercy. She thanked and prayed to Jacob for one act of mercy but we know that she was no less merciful herself.

Morrison offers one restorative possibility in the novel. In her novels she emphasizes on the importance of having a community of women. If in *Sula* one encounters a family run by powerful women in *Paradise,* one again encounters a strong community of women. These are, however, only two examples as in other novels one witnesses strong and important bonds forming between women. *A Mercy* too offers such possibility as in the farm of Jacob the un-mastered women form a community. A recuperative bond grows between Florens and Lina and through it, Morrison offers a way out. This is related to what O'Reilly calls 'othermothering'; "mothering expressed itself as both nurturance and work, and care of children was viewed as the duty of the larger community" (5). Othermothers (women who are not biological mothers) take care of children and community mothering involves taking care of the community in general. Both these acts of 'motherwork' are part of the process of healing both of the individual and the community. It is Lina who encourages Florens to embark upon the journey to find the blacksmith which is indeed taken on the literal, psychological and metaphorical plain together;

> This psychic journey of return, reconnection, and reclamation while directed to the spirit of a lost mother, is often initiated and overseen by an actual mother figure, a close female friend of the troubled woman who serves as an othermother for her... The othermother heals the woman by prompting her to take this journey of rememory and reconnection and assisting, comforting, and sustaining her as she does so. The me-ness that Morrison argues is central to the well-being therefore is either imparted to us as children through cultural bearing and nurturance or restored to us as adults through healing. And it is this me-ness that empowers the child to survive and resist. (O'Reilly 41)

The conclusion that I would like to draw at the end of this paper, that motherhood under slavery is a monumental effort on the part of the Black mothers who had to tide over the ghastly dehumanising effects of slavery. This act of tiding over if on one hand creates exemplary mothers, on the other this creates lesion for the children as well as the mothers lacerating both. However, Morrison does not end there by exposing the inhumanity that was slavery but moves ahead to suggest that with kindness and understanding one can achieve wholesomeness and redeem oneself in the face of greatest adversity. The trauma of broken mother-child can only be healed through journeys of 'rememory and reconnection' which are 'assisting, comforting, and sustaining'

## Notes

1. Morrison would go on to write two more novels after *A Mercy*, *Home* (2012) and *God Help the Child* (2014) before passing away in 2019. Of these, *God Help the Child* also addresses the troubled mother-child relation.
2. In this William Faulkner can be seen as Morrison's literary predecessor. Morrison wrote her postgraduate thesis on Virginia Woolf's and William Faulkner's treatment of the alienated in their fiction.
3. One may refer to Bhabha's well-known reading of colonial discursive politics in *The Location of Culture* (1994).

## Works Cited

Collins, Patricia Hill. *Black Feminist Thought: Knowledge, Consciousness, and the Politics of Empowerment.* New York: Routledge, 1991.

Hooks, Bell. *Yearning*: Race, Gender, and Cultural Politics. Boston: South End, 1990.

Morrison, Toni. *A Mercy.* New York: Alfred A. Knoff, 2008.

Moyers, Bill. "A Conversation with Toni Morrison." *Conversations with Toni Morrison.* Ed. Danille Taylor-Guthrie. 262-274. Jackson: University Press of Mississippi, 1994.

Naylor, Gloria. "A Conversation: Gloria Naylor and Toni Morrison." *Conversations with Toni Morrison.* Ed. Danille Taylor-Guthrie, pp. 188-217. Jackson: University Press of Mississippi, 1994.

O'Reilly, Andrea. *Toni Morrison and Motherhood: A Politics of the Heart.* Albany: State University of New York Press, 2004.

Stepto, Robert. "Intimate Things in Place: An Interview with Toni Morrison". *Conversations with Toni Morrison.* Ed. Danille Taylor-Guthrie, pp. 10-29. Jackson: University Press of Mississippi, 1994.

Tate, Claudia. "Toni Morrison" *Conversations with Toni Morrison.* Ed. Danille Taylor-Guthrie, pp. 156-170. Jackson: University Press of Mississippi, 1994.

SECTION THREE

# INNOCENCE, REALITIES AND RITUALISM

CHAPTER 7

# Desire, Disappointment and Derangement

## Pecola's Progression from Innocence to Insanity in *The Bluest Eye*

C Raju

IN HER novel *Four Girls at Cottage City*, Emma Dunham Kelley-Hawkins, one of the earliest Afro-American women writers talks about four young women: Vera, Allie, and sisters Jessie and Garnet. These four girls find a new uncontrolled freedom in their lives for the first time and go on vacation to a Massachusetts resort town. Very happily they treat themselves with sweets and enjoy the freedom. They experience women power afresh and decide to employ it effectively. During the course of this novel, we come across a conversation that provides a picture of the emotional turbulence these characters undergo. The conversation runs like this:

> "Well, we go to the theatre on an average of once a month,"
> "Yes, you bet we do," said Jessie, "if we do have to get seats in 'nigger heaven'"
> Garnett looked most indignant. "The idea!" she claimed, "I wouldn't say
> such a thing even in joke, if I were you, Jessie."

> "An'sure, I'm not saying it in joke. I'm deadly airnest, be jabbers." (81)

This conversation discusses about whether the act of going to the theatre is a personal prerogative or not in the American society of the late 19th century. The 'nigger heaven' refers to the theatre balcony reserved exclusively for African Americans. Garnett, one of the four girls, feels a kind of rage when she is faced with the reality whereas her sister Jessie is indignant of her. This 'reality' of keeping the Black twice-distanced from normal human relationships has dented their psyche deeply. For the African Americans, the country America itself feels like a 'nigger heaven'. Toni Morrison, in her writings, has just portrayed this trauma undergone by them in the spheres of race, gender, economy, family, childhood and adolescence i.e., in general, *life* itself. And her first novel *The Bluest Eye* is no exception.

Toni Morrison's writings are natural, from the heart and mostly self-experienced. She had the knack of telling a story in such a way that the readers could visualize. Her art of story-telling had been gradually nurtured from her childhood days. Her father told his children wonderful ghost stories. Many of them were so scary that his children would ask him to repeat the scariest part. Her mother, for her part, was a member of the local book club and this added to the literary imagination of Morrison. This training that Morrison was lucky to have during her early years later made her talk lucidly about the sufferings, sorrows, disappointments, betrayals, failures, violence, the disintegrating family structure due to poverty and infidelity, and racial abuse encountered by the African Americans in America. She could understand that for the African Americans,

America may have given them a place to stay but they are not fully free to lead a life of peace and calm. She engages herself in portraying the misery of the Black people that has evidences in her own life. While talking about her writings, she confesses:

> If anything I do, in the way of writing novels (or whatever I write), isn't about the village or the community or about you, then it is not about anything. I am not interested in indulging myself in some private, closed exercise of my imagination that fulfills only the obligation of my personal dreams-which is to say yes, the work must be political. ... It seems to me that the best art is political and you ought to make it unquestionably political and irrevocably beautiful at the same time. (Rootedness, 344-45)

Pecola Breedlove, the protagonist of the novel *The Bluest Eye*, is a highly complicated character who is almost docile in nature, yet dreamy. She lives in Lorain, Ohio, (also the birth place of Toni Morrison) first, with her parents and later with MacTeer's family. Peculiar in her wish and her constant actions, her name itself can be indicative of that inner personality. She appears very soft which leaves her endangered and imperilled. Morrison infuses in her two different invocations; one, a longing for love and the other the wish to disappear whenever she could no longer tolerate the violent fights between her parents. When these two invocations go unanswered, she slowly veers into a life of delusion, wishing for a pair of blue eyes, her third invocation. Without any break, she prays daily for her wish to be fulfilled. But Morrison gives a signal to the readers through the marigold whose seeds the MacTeer sisters

Claudia and Frieda plant for Pecola. Marigold is the flower of the dead in pre-Hispanic Mexico parallel to Lily in Europe. It is still used during the Day of the Dead celebrations.

At the outset itself, Morrison sprays character names with hidden meanings. Pecola's father is Cholly Breedlove (incidentally, Toni Morrison's baptized name is Chloe Anthony Wofford). His name itself is a misnomer because he never loves nor breeds love; on the contrary, he impregnates his own daughter. He burns down his house that leaves Pecola, her mother Pauline and her brother Sammy at the mercy of others. This incident is reminiscent of what happened to Morrison when she was just two years old. Her father George Wofford, a very hard-working man, could not pay $4 monthly rent for their house. The landlord asked them to leave as they could not pay. But Wofford refused. The landlord, in a fit of rage, burnt the house while her parents, she and her elder sister were inside. But fortunately, no one was injured. This incident had a lasting effect on Morrison's memory.

Unlike the four girls of Emma Dunham Kelley-Hawkins' novel, Pecola is weak and helpless. She could never enjoy the freedom the other four girls enjoyed. Nor could she attain the spiritual liberation and experience as the four girls. Pecola is distressed with a family that has neither love nor support for her, and her mind begins to disintegrate slowly. She often sees either her father violently quarrelling with her mother or mechanically having sex with his wife. Being only eleven years of age, she cannot withstand the severity of life.

Claudia MacTeer, the narrator of the story, and in whose house Pecola is lodged for the time being after their house is burned, is warned by her mother to be nice to the new girl.

> Mama had told us two days earlier that a "case" was coming—a girl who had no place to go. The county had placed her in our house for a few days until they could decide what to do, or, more precisely, until the family was reunited. We were to be nice to her and not fight. Mama didn't know "what got into people," but that old Dog Breedlove had burned up his house, gone upside his wife's head, and everybody, as a result, was outdoors. (16-17)

She is often traumatized by the other Black boys because of her dark skin and even the neighbourhood girls ill-treat her. When she was with her family, she made it a habit to look at the mirror frequently because she was upset and disappointed about her physical ugliness. Morrison says, "Long hours she sat looking in the mirror, trying to discover the secret of the ugliness, the ugliness that made her ignored or despised at school, by teachers and classmates alike."(45) Her only friends were the three sex workers who lived on the second floor of their house. She could feel love only with these three women who spoke to her without expecting anything. They even offered her candy, gave her clothes and narrated funny stories. After coming into the Master's family, she found the same love with Claudia and Frieda. She is possessed by the White standards of beauty. She had the notion that only white skin and the blue eyes could make her respected. For her, the possession of blue eyes would make her happy and recognized. The idea of the blue eye should have been prompted by Morrison's school mate who wished for blue eyes. In her conversation with Charles Ruas, she says:

> I looked at her and imagined her having them [blue eyes] and thought how awful that would be if she had gotten her prayer answered. I always thought she was beautiful. I began to write about a girl who wanted blue eyes and the horror of having the wish fulfilled; and also about the whole business of what is physical beauty and the pain of that yearning and wanting to be somebody else, and how devastating that was and yet part of all females who were peripheral in other people's lives. (95-96)

Morrison begins the novel in such a way that it is both verbally and visually haunting. At the outset itself Morrison seems to convey the fact that the novel is three layered which is visually portrayed by the way Dick and Jane reader is presented. The first layer of meaning is conveyed by this presentation: "Here is the house. It is green and white. It has a red door. It is very pretty. Here is the family. Mother, Father, Dick, and Jane live in the green-and-white house. (1). The second layer is presented in a more constricted way: Here is the house it is green and white it has a red door it is very pretty here is the family mother father dick and jane live in the green-and-white house they are very happy (1). The first layer, in which the sentence is complete and the description bright, represents the affluent White American society wherein everything is rosy. All is well and there is order, happiness and peace everywhere. The second layer, which has neither punctuation nor capital letters wherever necessary is the crystal-clear picture of Afro-American community. The dearth in the necessary punctuation and capital letters brings forth to the reader's eyes, the unequal, disorderly and struggling life of the African

Americans. The third layer, in which words had no spaces, is the pictorial representation of the disintegration in the spheres of morality, race, economy and gender. Incidentally, the choice of using William Elson and William Gray's Dick and Jane stories by Morrison is brilliant. The primer which originated in the 1930s became popular during the 1940s and 1950s. The primer venerated the white American middle-class family of three children Dick, Jane, and little sister Sally, a dog named Spot and a cat called Puff. The purpose of the primer was to depict the class and race difference prevalent during those years and emphasize the overriding thought of the day. By the way, it did not include the African American family till the late 1960s.

Before proceeding further into the analysis, a pertinent question pops up: what could have made Morrison title the novel in the superlative, *The Bluest Eye*? What could be the intent behind this and what does Morrison want to convey through this? May be this paper can proceed into finding the supposed answers which would lead us to the title of the paper. Normally what does blue stand for? We all know blue is one of the three primary colours. It is the colour which is usually connected with harmony, faithfulness, confidence, distance, infinity, the imagination, and emotionally, with sadness. Blues as a music genre had its beginnings in the Deep South of the United States around the 1860s primarily from the African Americans roots. Early traditional blues verses consisted of a single line repeated four times. The introduction of the blues is often dated to just after the ending of legalized slavery. It is associated with the newly acquired freedom of the former slaves. The term Blues may have come from "blue devils", meaning melancholy and sadness, an early use of the term in this sense is in George Colman's one-act farce *Blue Devils*. In the lyrics of the Blues music, words describe a depressed mood. Pecola's wish for the 'bluest eye' could indicate her wish for the early culmination of her suffering. Since 'blue' represents both the positivity and the negativity of the people of different nations, the longing for blue eyes can also indicate that Pecola is not sure what she really wants. Morrison has left it to us to decide whether she is positive or negative in nature.

Richard Wright, the critic, in his chapter 'Blue Print for Negro Writing' presents the inner conscience of a Black writer. In the chapter, he says:

> The Negro writer who seeks to function within his race as a purposeful agent has a serious responsibility. In order to do justice to his subject matter, in order to depict Negro life in all its manifold and intricate relationships, a deep, informed, and complex consciousness is necessary; a consciousness which draws for its strength upon the fluid lore of a great people, and molds this lore with the concepts that more and direct forces of history today. (102)

Toni Morrison's writings just reflect the nuances as envisaged by Wright. She possesses the complete and the 'complex consciousness' to describe the life of Pecola, hounded by her father, her friends and her race. Morrison again depicts the way she is surrounded by the community, not leaving any chance to lead an uneventful life.

Coming back to the novel, at the beginning itself we see how well the sisters Claudia and Frieda could move with Pecola. They treat her with affection and care and provide her with the dignity she always longed for. All things said and done, Pecola could not come out of the inherent longing for beauty. When Frieda gives her milk to drink in a Shirley Temple cup, she looks at it fondly. Toni Morrison beautifully captures this moment, "Frieda brought her four graham crackers on a saucer and some milk in a blue-and-white Shirley Temple cup. She was a long time with the milk, and gazed fondly at the silhouette of Shirley Temple's dimpled face." (19) The house in which she lived when she was with her parents was very uncouth and for the eleven-year-old Pecola it was an extension of herself. Describing the house, Toni Morrison writes,

> The plan of the living quarters was as unimaginative as a first-generation Greek landlord could contrive it to be. The large "store" area was partitioned into two rooms by beaverboard planks that did not reach the ceiling. There was a living room, which the family called the front room, and the bedroom, where all the living was done. In the front room were two sofas, an upright piano, and a tiny artificial Christmas tree which had been there, decorated and dust laden, for two years. The bedroom had three beds: a narrow iron bed for Sammy, fourteen years old, another for Pecola, eleven years old, and a double bed for Cholly and Mrs Breedlove. In the center of the bedroom, for the even distribution of heat, stood a coal stove. Trunks, chairs, a small end table, and a cardboard "wardrobe" closet were placed around the walls. The kitchen was in the back of this apartment, a separate room. There were no bath facilities. Only a toilet bowl, inaccessible to the eye, if not the ear, of the tenants. (34-35)

Adding to that was the physical ugliness she inherited from her father. Pecola was obsessed with it always. Morrison writes,

> The eyes, the small eyes set closely together under narrow foreheads. The low, irregular hairlines, which seemed even more irregular in contrast to the straight, heavy eyebrows which nearly met. Keen but crooked noses, with insolent nostrils. They had high cheekbones, and their ears turned forward. Shapely lips which called attention not to themselves but to the rest of the face. (38-39)

Slowly, her hallucination comes to set in. A kind of bizarre wish comes to haunt her. The inferior inner self begins to move into delirium. Pecola starts to believe in the fact that if she had been endowed with such and such physical attributions, she would have been beautiful. She firmly believes that people would not have made fun of her considering her beauty. She fantasizes:

> It had occurred to Pecola some time ago that if her eyes, those eyes that held the pictures, and knew the sights—if those eyes of hers were different, that is to say, beautiful, she herself would be different. Her teeth were good, and at least her nose was not big and flat like some of those who were thought so cute. If she looked different, beautiful, maybe Cholly would be different, and Mrs Breedlove too. Maybe they'd say, "Why, look at pretty-eyed Pecola. We mustn't do bad things in front of those pretty eyes. (46)

This makes her wish for the bluest eyes daily. She earnestly feels that her prayers would be answered and she would be relieved of the pain of being the ugliest girl. She daydreams that people would not do her any harm and they would accord her the proper dignity that any human being deserves. She is so naïve, immature and unsophisticated that she is not ashamed of dreaming about her eyes.

> Each night, without fail, she prayed for blue eyes. Fervently, for a year she had prayed. Although somewhat discouraged, she was not without hope. To have something as wonderful as that happen would take a long, long time. Thrown, in this way, into the binding conviction that only a miracle could relieve her, she would never know her The Bluest Eye beauty. She would see only what there was to see: the eyes of other people. (46-47)

Pecola's sensitivity is further dented when she befriends a girl named Maureen Peal. She hails from a rich family and has light skin which is regarded highly by other African Americans. She has long brown hair which has been kept in two braids. The other girls consider her as rich as White girls. Her clothes, leather shoes with buckles, fluffy sweaters, coloured knee socks with white borders, and brown velvet coat trimmed in white rabbit fur put off all other girls. Let us see how their conversation goes. Let us also see the reaction of Pecola.

> "I just moved here. My name is Maureen Peal. What's yours?"
>
> "Pecola."
>
> "Pecola? Wasn't that the name of the girl in *Imitation of Life?*"

> "I don't know. What is that?"
> "The picture show, you know. Where this mulatto girl hates her mother cause, she is Black and ugly but then cries at the funeral. It was real sad. Everybody cries in it. Claudette Colbert too."
> "Oh." Pecola's voice was no more than a sigh.

Pecola's innocence and the eventual fall into madness can be seen from her association with the pedophile Soaphead Church. It is masterly of Morrison to name him so. There is of course no meaning in his first name 'Soaphead' and his second name 'Church' indicates how diametrically opposite is he to Christian faith. He claims himself to be spiritualist, and convinces others that he has the ability to interpret dreams. His pose as a miracle worker makes Pecola believe in his powers. She confesses to him her wish for blue eyes. People normally approach him to seek three things love, health and money. He understands that she wants something from him. He asks: "What can I do for you, my child?" (173) Pecola is unsure whether he could satisfy her wish because it is different. With a little bit of hesitation, she says, "Maybe. Maybe you can do it for me." (173) She asks him if he can grant her the wish of possessing blue eyes.

> "I can't go to school no more. And I thought maybe you could help me."
> "Help you how? Tell me. Don't be frightened."
> "My eyes."
> "What about your eyes?"
> "I want them blue." (174)

Soaphead first does not know how to react. He reminds the reader of the character Raju in R.K. Narayan's novel *The Guide*. Raju, a tour guide turned criminal is considered a holy man by the innocent villagers and they expect him to fast for twelve days to bring rain to the parched village. Raju also unashamedly undergoes this penance which is nothing but deceit. Soaphead wants to confess at first that he does not have the powers to grant Pecola's wish. But the original Soaphead's character surges ahead. He does not like his landlady Bertha Reese's dog and wants to kill it. Hence, he sprinkles poison on some meat and asks Pecola to offer it to the dog. He convinces her that if the dog behaved strangely, she could get her wish.

> Take this food and give it to the creature sleeping on the porch. Make sure he eats it. And mark well how he behaves. If nothing happens, you will know that God has refused you. If the animal behaves strangely, your wish will be granted on the day following this one. (175)

Pecola is aghast to see the dog die and she runs away. Claudia and Frieda plan to help Pecola by praying and sacrificing. But Pecola's mind is completely deranged now. Pecola begins to talk with an imaginary friend. The imaginary friend is accused by Pecola for being jealous of her blue eyes. In complete mental disarray, Pecola does not understand why people don't come near her. Claudia starts to describe Pecola's madness. The novel ends with Claudia's words:

> This soil is bad for certain kinds of flowers. Certain seeds it will not nurture, certain fruits it will not bear, and when the land kills of its own volition, we acquiesce and say the victim had no right to live. We are wrong, of course, but

> it doesn't matter. It's too late. At least on the edge of my town, among the garbage and the sunflowers of my town, it's much, much, much too late. (206)

Morrison has created Pecola's character to stand as a representation for the whole Black community, particularly the Black women. The portrayal of her ugliness is a pictorial presentation of the life of the unfortunate African Americans. Pecola's directionless roaming at the edge of town worries her community, reminding them of the ugliness and hatred that they have tried to repress. Jane Kuenz sums up the life of Pecola:

> The inability to make her eyes go away prompts Pecola's final disappearing act: The ugliness of her entire body is dissolved in and absolved by the blue eyes only she and her new friend can see. Her breakdown at the end of the novel is the last in the series of instances in which boundaries marking the space between inside and outside, self and other, sense and nonsense are broken, removed, or simply no longer perform their tasks. As the novel's prefatory Dick-and-Jane story turns from order to chaos with the gradual removal of punctuation and spacing, so too does the erasure of Pecola's body and sexuality lead to her madness and isolation. (421)

She stands as an example of the Black suffering in general and Black women in particular and the reader is lucky to see her mind degenerate because she no longer can have the sense to feel the nonsense around her. Thus, she is saved.

## Works Cited

Kelley-Hawkins, Emma Dunham. Four Girls at Cottage City. New York: Oxford University Press, 1988.

Kuenz, Jane. "The Bluest Eye: Notes on History, Community and Black Female Subjectivity." *African American Review*, vol. 27, no. 3, 1993.

Morrison, Toni. The Bluest Eye. Vintage Books, 1970

—. "Rootedness: The Ancestor as Foundation." Black Women Writers (1950-1980) A Critical Evaluation. Ed. Maria Evans. Anchor Books, 1984.

Ruas, Charles. Conversations with American Writers. Knopf, 1985.

Wright, Richard. "Blue Print for Negro Writing" Within the Circle: An Anthology of African American Literary Criticism from the Harlem Renaissance to the Present. Ed. Angelyn Mitchell. Duke University Press, 1994.

CHAPTER 8

# Critical Exposition of *Playing in the Dark*

## A New Reading of *Beloved*

Cyrine Kortas

TO DEAL with (in)visibility in a racially segregated America one has to go beyond the mere dictionary definition of being coloured, because black skinned Americans have always been slipping from the very country's consciousness. The first act of shadowiness was when the American constitution remained silent over the issue of slavery and declared Black Americans one third of a person. Hence, their invisibility is due to interconnected historical, social, economic and cultural factors that perpetuated till the second half of the twentieth century to prove that their neglect was not due to their intrinsic worth as human beings but due to their skin colour that prevented them from assimilating into American society; they remained at the threshold of a society they contributed to in the making of its body and soul.

In fact, the invisibility of the black self was a controversial issue among early nineteenth century American intellectuals and thinkers who held different views on what had caused it and how to redeem the black self and secure its visibility in society, among whom we can mention Booker T. Washington (1856-1915). Blaming slavery, Washington asserted that his people's idleness and lack of initiative were direct consequences of years and years of bondage. Though Washington was disapproving of political activism and called for conciliation and gradualism that won him his people's criticism, he was among the first Black American thinkers to draw light to the issue of people of colour's invisibility and marked the massive culmination of Black Americans' efforts to regain their visibility, lost through centuries of oppression, injustice, and exploitation.

For decades, the issue of slavery and its lingering consequences on black Americans remained an important concern among intellectuals, thinkers and artists. Though it was abolished centuries ago, slavery haunted the Black people's daily life, artistic creations and philosophical interest. Starting with the slave narratives of Frederick Douglass, Harriet Tubman, to name a few, slavery found ways to regenerate itself in the Black people's works being literary or critical addressing the atrocities befalling the race. In this vein comes Toni Morrison's critical work *Playing in the Dark* that influenced her writing of *Beloved.*

The purpose of this paper is to shed light on a little-known side of Toni Morrison who, to many, is visible as an author, but invisible as a critic. This paper aims to bring simultaneously her critical and literary works to dissipate the long gloom that surrounded the African Americans since the dawn of slavery and centuries after its abolishment.

"I want to draw a map," (Morrison, *Playing in the Dark* 3) so begins Toni Morrison's first piece of criticism that would further foreground her stature not only as a writer but also as a literary critic. In 1992, in the aftermath of her Pulitzer Prize for literature, Toni Morrison "contributes significantly to the debate about the canon of American literature in general and, in particular," (Wallinger 115) the overshadowed African American contribution to which she refers to in her work *Playing in the Dark* "dark, abiding, signing Africanist presence" (6). In the opening pages of her work, Morrison states the purpose of her critical endeavor to be "... an investigation into the ways in which a non-white, African like (or Africanist) presence or persona was constructed in the United States, and the imaginative uses this fabricated presence served" (6). The introduction draws attention to two major functions of the critique. One is the mapping of the Africanist presence that has been rendered invisible for centuries, and second is the understanding of the reasons behind such shadowy presence.

Morrison's mapping of the Black presence is divided into three acts. The first section, entitled "Black Matters," accentuates the shadowy presence of Black characters in American canon literature as it's presence is not written for Black people, "No more Uncle Tom's Cabin was for Uncle Tom to be read or persuaded by" (16). The second chapter discusses the New World as the land of opportunity and the locus of freedom. Yet, this freedom and this opportunity seem to be race-conscious, while canonical literature as defined by Morrison should be "universal and race-free" (12). The final part of the book, "Disturbing Nurses and the Kindness of Sharks," is a call for disturbing the calm waters and bringing to the forefront the compelling subject of the Africanist presence. She chooses to do so by discussing Willa Cather's *Sapphira and the Slave Girl.* Though another slave narrative was mentioned in *Uncle Tom's Cabin*, Morrison focuses on Cather's work epitomizing the "silence of four hundred years [that] leaps out of the novel's void and out of the void of historical discourse on slave relationships and pain" (22). To rectify this silence, Morrison wrote *Beloved*, a revisited slave narrative via which she aims to bring voice to the Africanist self and assert its position in the historical discourse. To tell her people's stories and fight their wars, Morrison engages in mapping matters of race by challenging the "silence and evasion [that] have historically ruled the literary discourse" (9). The implemented metaphor of a map resets borders and limits, re-reads history and re-pens the Black American character. It resets borders by permitting the slave character to cross over and reach out for freedom. It re-reads history by asserting the mobility and agency of the slave characters long depicted as submissive and passive and presents the slave characters under a new image that matters to the Black American reader. It is in this vein that the paper studies the character of Sethe the runaway slave who is an Africanist presence that shapes the novel and the artist's identity.

*Playing in the Dark* alleges that Black American characters have been imposed an absence to the expense of a contribution to American identity. Hence, the work's goal is to uncover an Africanist visible position. It is in this context that *Beloved* stands as a practice of such an endeavor as it permits the author to employ "the ways [that] transform aspects of [her] social grounding into aspects of language, and the ways [to] tell other stories, fight secret wars, himn out all sorts of debates blanketed in the text" (Morrison 4). The novel offers suggestion for altering the position of Black American characters in collective memory and canonical literature by providing an exceptional reflection on the dark history of slavery and redefining the North's abolitionist reputation by emerging from the dark labyrinth of a restless spirit that beholds the atrocities and horrors of crossing over. Morrison's interest in slavery as a premise for Africanist acknowledgment reflects a John Hope Franklin's call "[w]e should never forget slavery. We should talk about it every morning and every day of the year to remind this country that there is an enormous gap between its practices and its professions" (Weinburg par3). Addressing slavery remains a relevant topic century after its abolition as it is the very reason behind the invisibility of African Americans.

Toni Morrison's *Beloved* stands as a "compelling" narrative that depicts the horrors of slavery befalling a Black American woman. Building on the slave narrative of her ancestors, Morrison retells her people's story asserting the difference that slavery is a past that can never be put to rest, accentuating its physical and psychological scars. Set in Bluestone Road, Cincinnati, 1873, the novel depicts some slaves' attempts to freedom, deftly recording their crossing journeys and standing as a "true [revisiting of the] history of African American slavery" (Bloom 7). True to a long history of slave narrative, *Beloved* depicts its female protagonist struggling to reach Ohio to finally embrace freedom. Yet, when moving in place, the past holds her back making it difficult for her to forget the horrors of bondage. Sethe's journey proves to be not only physical but also inward. "Journeying into the self," (Davies) seems to accompany the journey into land. Hence, *Beloved* is not just an escape into freedom but also a journey into exploring and defining the Black self to bring it out of its shadow and to reconcile with its past demons. The characters' experiences of movement do therefore, weave a labyrinth of broken dreams and pained selves.

Crossing borders and confronting the chains of man and the powers of nature are recurrent images enlivening slave narrative to assert that the escape into freedom was a thorny path. True to a long tradition that did not waver to focus on the horrors of the journey, Morrison starts her novel with the origins of slavery by addressing that the Middle Passage evokes images of "men without skin" (*Beloved* 210). The atrocity of the Middle Passage and the pain and grief it inflicted on captive Africans when being sold to the new world seems to have lingered and marked the race's collective memory to find way into Morrison's writing that works as a reminder in order not to forget the sacrifices of the race. The image of a ship stiffed with Black slaves forced to bear the wrath of nature and the whip of the White man stand as "a rememory" in African American literature. Yet, this image is set in contrast with another image associated with the Ohio River. While crossing the Atlantic from Africa to the New World stands as an acute memory of bondage and dependence, crossing the Ohio River asserts an embrace of liberty, a rebirth. In their escape to freedom, runaway slaves considered one major route to reach the North that of crossing the river, the border between a free North and the plantations in the South. It seems that Morrison elaborated both images as if asserting that the Black man's destiny is that of liberation and freedom. According to Mathew Salafia, the Ohio River functions as "a borderland of slavery and freedom" and "a conduit of movement," (43) for runaway slaves. His words coincide with The Northwest Ordinance Act of 1787 that declared the Northern side of the Ohio River free. In the slaves' collective memory, the river stands as their ticket to the free world. Morrison's characters are no exception.

The newly freed Sethe is reminiscing about her journey from the Sweet Home plantation in Kentucky to 124 Bluestone Road, Cincinnati, Ohio. The novel is about a slave mother who crosses the Ohio River hoping to grant her children a better, freer and safer life. Actually, the plot of the narrative echoes numerous crossings taking place in the river setting, becoming a place of reunion in which Black slaves were able to share their stories and trace common history of pain and grief as well as aspirations of hopes and dreams. The character's crossing brings to the modern reader the image of the slave mother Margaret Garner who fled the South and crossed the frozen Ohio on foot, (Salafia 67) becoming as such "the historical analogue of the plot of *Beloved*" (Rushdy 39). In the image of her ancestor, Morrison draws a picture of a pregnant slave who refuses her master's physical and emotional abuse and humiliation and runs away, hoping to grant her still unborn child a better life. Such hope grants her determination not "to die on the wrong side of the river" (*Beloved* 90). Other characters than Sethe, such as Paul D, Halle, Sixo, to name a few, "made up [their] mind[s] about what to do with the heart that started beating the minute [they] crossed the Ohio River" (*Beloved* 147). The liberating forces that the river is associated with in the slaves' imagination present it as the locus of rebirth and the journey for it as a sacred pilgrimage that asserts the characters' redemption of the abuses of the past.

Knowing the possible dangers that the slaves run in order to reach the river, Morrison pens a narrative marked by a tight sense of suspense. Sethe, Paul D, Baby Suggs, and many other slaves planned their journeys northward and took the necessary precautions so as not to be caught. Such image of slaves who would create plans and schemes is meant to contradict the very classical stereotype of slaves as being human cattle, mindless labour force as the Whites wanted to depict them. Agency and mobility are intertwined in the depiction of Morrison's runaway slaves. In search of freedom and "better lives," (Yohe 212) characters in *Beloved* are engaged in weekly trips, secretly leaving the plantation and meeting with the Thirty Mile Woman who would guarantee their escape. These female characters not only revolt against their destiny of abuse and exploitation but also against the limitations of their gender. Being interested in the women question and the untold history of Black female slaves, Morrison contributes to the slave narrative by focusing on different journeys taken by different slave women who were in search of freedom and self. Baby Suggs, Sethe and Denver are all slaves who embark on this holy journey to cross the holy Ohio River and be baptized into freedom and liberation. While Baby Suggs reaches 124 Cincinnati as an old woman, "whose heart started beating" the minute she crossed the river, Sethe is a traumatized slave who gives birth to her baby girl on the route. Denver, on the other hand, crosses the river as a newly born girl who carries the race's hope. These women's journeys present the slaves' escapes as an act of resistance and rebellion.

Whipped by cowhide, mammary raped, and identified as a breeding animal, Sethe tells her story, depicting the oppression she was subject to that drove her to run away. Sethe decides to escape torture and humiliation and take the thorny path many other African brethrens took in quest of a decent and more human life. Reaching "124" a temporary safe home, Sethe reconnects with her family members as they were separated by slavery. Though short-lived, Sethe's new life testifies to the importance of the journey she took. She inhales the new life replete with possibilities, hopes, and dreams. She "had claimed herself," writes Morrison (*Beloved* 95).

A gothic, gloomy atmosphere reigns over the first pages of the novel. Such an atmosphere is generated by the depiction of the runaway slave's house in the outskirts of Cincinnati, Ohio. After crossing the river, Sethe finds herself and her newly born baby girl in a shabby shelter that became their lodging for over 18 years. This reunion and this freedom would not have been possible had Sethe remained a submissive slave in the Sweet Home plantation. Taking this mother and her child to the shores of safety, this crossing grants them a new life. Interestingly, however, the onset depiction of the house contradicts the importance associated with the place, "124 WAS SPITEFUL. Full of a baby's venom," (*Beloved* 4) a house "packed to its rafters with some dead Negro's grief" (*Beloved* 6). The grief that surrounds the house is an indication of unfulfillment. Driven by an urging desire to be free, Sethe survives the atrocities of slavery, the risks and pains of crossing the river to embrace liberty and freedom. However, this survival remains at the threshold of her fulfillment. Pain and hurt still mark her existence, chaining her to the demons of the past.

Actually, Morrison's protagonist is thrust into a Northern crib that does not seem to have healed her wounds or provided her with a feeling of inner peace or a sense of security. The twenty-eight days of pursuing her dream of liberty, of planning, sacrificing, of pain and hurt could not render her happy or satisfied as something from the past remains to mar her present. The memories and traumas of the past find their way to shadow her happiness and render her freedom invisible as other chains come to replace those of slavery. The newly free Black woman is a traumatized person unable to lead a normal life with her child as the fetters of slavery seem to callously smother her every dream of happiness and liberty, even now that she is miles and years away from the plantation. The pitiful memory of slavery is the ghost that haunts her life.

The novel gives us access to a richly described world of a gloomy house, painful memories, and broken dreams. This description is marked by an in-betweenness as the protagonist is torn between her dreams of freedom and liberty and love and family on the one hand, and the reality of her current situation in the outskirts of the American North on the other hand. Similar to its protagonist, the text is itself unfixed in terms of narration, haunted by memories and flashbacks. Quivering as a ghost, the past keeps haunting the text. Slavery haunts both Sethe and her creator. Similar to her ancestors, Morrison is trying to heal the wounds of the past; this is clear in the voice that speaks in the text that cannot distance itself from the historical dilemmas of the past whose consequences still linger in the author's present. Such in-betweenness experienced by both Sethe and Morrison results in what Derrida coined as text hauntology.

Derrida's term of hauntology was first coined in *Specters of Marx* in 1993. It describes the instable indefinable ontology. In other words, "our here and now" is never bare and alone. Our presence is haunted by intangible webs of the past and other. Derrida writes that if writing is what puts the simulacrum into play, then the simulacrum bears force, this force "ceaselessly dislocates identity, especially the identity of the[speaking] I" (361/325).

The simulacrum gains force from the past that seeks to find ways to recreate itself anew. The past's endless ways to emerge made Derrida assert that "here, now, yes, believe me, I believe in ghosts". Slavery becomes Morrison's ghost, marring the present and deepening its wounds. Such recreation grants the text a gothic dimension that further accentuates the struggle of an old self that fails to recreate itself anew. The novel's gothic dimension is undeniable, asserting that there is a concomitant move toward contemporary psychological and political elements of Gothic literature. As early as 2000, Chris Baldick and Robert Mighall were already proposing that criticism "has tended to reinvent [the Gothic] in the image of its own projected intellectual goals of psychological 'depth' and 'political' subversion, ... presenting [contemporary] Gothic literature as a kind of revolt".(267-268)

To explore its psychological depth and political subversion, contemporary Gothic literature has taken a highly visual experience of re-exploring memories of the past to highlight modern traumas and dilemmas as escaping bondage and carrying the struggle of one's ancestors for freedom and recognition. This explains Morrison's interest and revival of tradition of slave narratives. The interest stems from the very question of whether the slaves' freedom was limited to a change in place. In other words, was slavery connoted to the limitation of the individual to space or did it stretch deeper to impose fetters on their memories, dreams and hopes?

Once freed, Sethe is faced with a new dilemma, the haunting and crippling "rememories," as she calls them, memories of past suffering and grief over act of unwilling infanticide. As much she strives to block these memories from emerging, keeping them "at bay," (*Beloved* 69) as much they resist forgetfulness and preclude her present life. What seems as a self-defense mechanism turns to be the very reason of the protagonist's trauma and pain. Her refusal to journey back to her past and "...beat back the past," (*Beloved* 70) seem to pain her even more. Sethe asserts that "I took one journey and I paid for the ticket ... it cost too much" (*Beloved* 15). The cost is the facing of her worries, memories and past demons that deny her the joy of embracing her freedom. Morrison affirms that "her brain was not interested in the future. Loaded with the past and hungry for me, it left no room to imagine, let alone plan for the next day" (*Beloved* 70). Unable to move forward or to let go of her past, Sethe, as many other runaway slaves, remained at the threshold of freedom, stagnated and haunted by the wounds of the past. It becomes evident that the physical journey is not the guarantee to a slave's freedom, matching a Morrisonian idea that "geographical relocation alone does not suffice," (Yohe 213) for the runaway slave to take on complete liberation.

Delving deeper into the recesses of her soul, Sethe has to relive all her pains and reconcile with her past to be finally able to call herself free. While crossing the river took her twenty-eight days, reconciling with her past took years and still she could not overcome the pain and grief. Remembering the past, she tells Paul D about the boys that whipped her, repeating in a dramatic manner "... they tool my milk" (*Beloved* 17). Confronting her painful memories, Sethe is laying bare a past of intolerable humiliation and agony that stripped her from her humanity. Such agony is meant to explore the invisible side of slavery, a side that a twenty-century Black American can relate to though slavery has been abolished for centuries. The novel does indeed question the very notion of Black Americans' freedom and lay bare the deeply rooted legacy of slavery that finds its way to mar the existence of modern Black Americans.

*Beloved* is a novel that puts under scrutiny various elements of the slave narrative. While past narratives explore the physical act of crossing over to a better freer place, the work under study complicates the journey when associating the physical journey with another crossing, the emotional journey Sethe is set on, which proves to be more threatening and painful. In fact, Morrison believes that an internal journey for the individual to "whole again" is much needed to realize one's self. Actually, physical and psychological crossings seem to overlap in *Beloved* attesting the dilemmas the Black self had to endure to finally become visible in a society that overshadowed its existence and contribution to the making of the American saga, not only in history books but also in the collective memory and artifacts of culture. Through this novel, Morrison is paying tribute to her ancestors whose escapes were stories of endurance and challenge.

The critically acclaimed 1987 novel *Beloved* came to crown a critical endeavor that presented Morrison as a visible critic who asserted the need for revisiting American history and re-read the Africanist presence in its canonical literature that the racist attitudes of the country tried to veil and contain. Refusing oblivion, slavery, the reminder of invisibility, is reinvented in the novel to remind the author, her people, and the nation in general about the wounds of the past that are to be healed and redeemed through memory. Memory becomes a voyage in time and place to face the past and heal its traumas, without which the Black self cannot assert its presence and make proof of its visibility.

## Works Cited

Baldick, Chris and Robert Mighall. "Gothic Criticism." *A Companion to the Gothic*. Ed. David Punter. Blackwell Publishers, 2000, pp. 209-28.

Bloom, Harold, ed. *Bloom's Guide: Toni Morrison's Beloved*. Chelsea and House Publishers, 2004.

Davies, Carole Boyce. *Black Women, Writing and Identity: Migrations of the Subject*. Routledge, 2003.

Derrida, Jacques. *Spectres of Marx*. Trans. Peggy Kamuf. Routledge, 2006.

Morrison, Toni. *Beloved*. Plume PG, 1988.

—. *Playing in the Dark: Whiteness and the Literary Imagination*. Vintage Books, 1993.

Rushdy, Ashraf H.A. "Daughters Signifyin(g) History: The Example of Toni Morrison's *Beloved*." *Toni Morrison's Beloved: A Casebook*. Ed. William L. Andrews and Nelie Y. Mckay. New York: Oxford University Press, 1999, pp. 37-66.

Salafia, Mathew. *Slavery's Borderland: Freedom and Bondage along the Ohio River*. Pennsylvania University Press, 2013.

Wallinger, Hanna. "Toni Morrison's Literary Criticism." *The Cambridge Companion to Toni Morrison*. Ed. Justine Tally. Cambridge University Press, 2007, pp. 115-124.

Washington, Booker, T. *Up from Slavery.* Dell Publishing Co., Inc., 1965.

Weinberg, Carl R. "Antebellum Slavery." *Organization of American Historians Magazine of History.* Oxford Journals. Arizona State University. 2 April 2009. Accessed 10 June 2021. http://maghis.oxfordjournals.org.ezproxy1.lib.asu.edu

Yohen, Kristen. "Migration." *The Toni Morrison Encyclopedia.* Ed.

Elizabeth Ann Beaulieu. Greenwood Press, 2003, pp. 200-20.

CHAPTER 9

# Toni Morrison's Writings

## A New Model for African American Literature

Nitesh Narnolia

"Life is life. Precious."

– Toni Morrison in *Song of Solomon*

TONI MORRISON'S works examines and reexamines the essence of life. Through her characters, she explores the various aspects of life and celebrates life with her narrative audience which she has created for her novels. Her characters are courageous as she tells the stories which the readers don't wish to relate with but are compelled to do so. She writes as a Black woman whose voice is still undervalued in postcolonial and postmodern America and balances her personal and political life to portray African-American socio-cultural history. She narrates powerful stories while using poetic language and specific narrative techniques, which will be discussed later in the chapter.

In 1993, Toni Morrison became the first African-American woman to obtain the Nobel Prize in Literature which made the Swedish Academy describe her as a writer "who, in novels characterized by visionary force and poetic import, gives life to an essential aspect of American reality" (Beaulieu ix). Though Morrison was already a writer of international repute, her recognition as an intellectual grew after the Nobel Prize. Toni Morrison can be considered an 'intellectual property' for her contribution in the literary world. This article will look at Toni Morrison as a Black feminist, as a womanist and as a postcolonial critic while evaluating the use of language and narrative techniques in her novels in order to exemplify Toni Morrison as an 'intellectual property' of the world of literature.

Novels by Toni Morrison can be studied from a feminist point of view as they encounter the established norms of race, gender and class through their language and narrative techniques. As it is seen, the language is mainly 'male-centered' and supports masculinity and male traits. In literary works, language is anticipated to be authoritative, critical and rational. Contrary to this, women characters are demonstrated as incompetent of proper verbal expressions and more dependent on emotional and irrational expressions. So, the language of the text is largely masculine. Johnnie M. Stover writes in *The Toni Morrison Encyclopedia*: "A woman's approach to language is not meant to overpower or to conquer, but strives to build bridges of understanding and inclusion in a society where her voice, in order to be heard, must resonate with difference" (Beaulieu 13). Hence, the language of a woman differs from that of a man. This difference in language is not because of the difference in gender, but because a woman is considered an artefact of socio-cultural surrounding of a male dominated society where she has been molded through oppression and silence. This oppression of woman becomes severe with the Black women in American culture, which although has been reflected by many writers in their works, but only Black women writers do more justice. This representation of Black women has resulted into exclusion of Black women writers from the mainstream literary traditions.

Toni Morrison has used humor and songs as two narrative techniques to depict Black women's oppression and resistance in her works. The depiction of resistance in Morrison's novels emphasizes on locating and relocating of Black life, particularly the Black women in America. Morrison's novel, *The Bluest Eye* depicts the suppression of the African Americans who are enforced to identify themselves as per Western values of beauty. One of the characters, Claudia MacTeer narrates Pecola Breedlove's devastation while recollecting their childhoods. MacTeer shares the story of Pecola which she has seen as a Black woman from the periphery of the society. Her language relies upon the Black practice of gospels and blues music, thus blurring the boundaries between poetry and prose. The stylistic organization of *The Bluest Eye* and the "construction of characters support the woman's unique understanding and use of alternative communicative devices" (Beaulieu 14). It tells how blues is used and lived by Morrison's women characters. Mrs MacTeer, Claudia's mother, occasionally starts singing the blues while working around in the house. The life of the three sex workers China, Poland and Miss Marie have also been depicted through blues music which blurs the phallocentric traits of language. Hence, this singing of women illustrates gender and class oppression in the novel.

Morrison's *Sula* addresses the relationship between women through the relationship of Sula Peace and Nel Wright. The novel depicts women with nurturing, creative and destructive powers. Eva Peace is the woman-God in *Sula*. Things become exactly what she names them. So, Morrison makes Eva "naming all stray boys as 'Dewey' irrespective of their race and class" (Beaulieu 15). Hence, there is no difference between Black and White stray boys. Johnnie M. Stover writes, "Morrison not only deconstructs color here, she reduces the importance of maleness through her codification of these male figures under the control of Eva Peace" (Beaulieu 15). In the novel *Song of Solomon*, the male characters have been depicted as egocentric and narcissistic while the women characters arise as nurtures and raconteurs. One of the women characters Pilate Dead works as a link between the physical and the spiritual world as she recreates history and reunites herself through fragments of memories she carts with her. Through Pilate, Morrison rejects the traditional norms set for women. It can be reflected as a story of "the Black woman's sacrifice to protect and ensure the community's ancestral memory" (Beaulieu 17). Other novels by Morrison, *Beloved* and *Jazz* also focus on the survival of Black women and nurture the Black heritage.

Thus, Morrison is a Black feminist who has carved the strong Black women characters in her novels who carry themselves in a dignified way, who nurture the Black heritage and traditions while being a part of the Western society, who share strong bonds with each other and who demonstrate the oppression Black women have to go through in the American society and culture.

Along with feminism, Toni Morrison can also be placed within the domain of Womanism. Black women authors including Toni Morrison have illustrated the principles of womanism in their works which has been grounded by Alice

Walker in the preface of *In Search of Our Mothers' Gardens* (1983). Walker's philosophy focuses on "how racist, classist and sexist power structure of American society disempower African-American women. In womanist works which are often structured as bildungsroman" (Beaulieu 39), the female character sets forth on a literal or psychological journey confronting literal or psychological enslavement to achieve personal freedom. Though, womanism rejects separatism and encourages both men and women to create ideal communities that are away from gender, class and racial differences, as Patricia Collins in *Black Feminist Thought: Knowledge, Consciousness, and the Politics of Empowerment* (1990) argues, "[B]lack women's struggles are part of a wider struggle for human dignity and empowerment" (37). Still, when womanism challenges oppressive power structures to create a space for woman, bell hooks claims that "womanism is not sufficiently linked to a tradition of radical political commitment to struggle and change" (Collins 182).

*The Bluest Eye*, *Sula* and *Beloved* are novels that exemplify how Morrison encirclements and encounters womanist principles in her works. Generally, the womanist voyage towards self-esteem and empowerment begins with the depiction of Black women characters trapped in oppressive and antagonistic environment that obstruct their growth. Thus, Morrison sets her novels in such settings where the characters fight against societal forces of race, class and gender domination which demoralize the individual power and free will of the Black women characters. In *The Bluest Eye*, Pecola's conviction about having blue eyes for an improved life shatters in the abandoned store in Lorain, Ohio. Her experience within the store exemplifies a miniature of violence and subjugation, Pecola escapes this ugly world when she moves in with the MacTeer family. But there also, she is deprived of maternal nourishment. Thus, Pecola finds no place to go or to grow. In her novel *Sula,* Morrison moderates the unfavorable atmosphere's disparaging potential by providing the protagonist the authority to escape. The protagonist, Sula Peace wishes "to create an individual self; however, both the society and the family threaten this goal" (Beaulieu 40). As Sula was determined to create her own identity, she rebels against the oppression by escaping to Eva Peace's attic. Morrison builds a more complex womanist space in *Beloved* through the depiction of women characters' skirmish between governing and dwindling prisoner to the places they inhabit in order to develop their self-worth. Sethe Suggs attempts "to make Sweet Home her own space by gathering flowers for the kitchen. However, she cannot create a safe niche for herself as Schoolteacher turns the Sweet Home into a space that breaks Sethe's body, mind and family" (Beaulieu 40). Thus, Toni Morrison as a womanist depicts a range of characters such as Pecola, Sula and Sethe who inspire Black women in America for self-creation and exploration.

The term postcolonial writer is used for "Anglophone and Francophone writers from postcolonial nations which are generally termed as the Third World nations" (Beaulieu 30). However, this term can also be used for African-American writers who experience a kind of colonial history of suppression. While using the term postcolonial in American context, the descendants of African diaspora can be looked at where Toni Morrison emerges as a strong postcolonial writer through her depiction of the legacy of African diaspora and Middle Passage. Toni Morrison's novels, when viewed through the postcolonial lens, explores the idea of home and establishes the notion that "home is unstable topography between protected private space and vulnerable public space threatened by the American colony's destructive desire to reduce Black bodies to chattel" as explained by James M. Ivory (Beaulieu 30). This idea of home has led Morrison to explore individual identity and self-worth. This notion of identity and self has been demonstrated through sexual politics in the novel *Sula* where both the public and private space of home is relatively disconcerting. The struggle of Sula Peace and Nel Wright for their individual identities can be considered akin to the questions of derivation linked to the dislocated history of African-American slaves. In the novel *Sula,* the question of embracing or rejecting 'home' within "the context of one's sexual identity is a question that individuals face within the postcolonial world" (Beaulieu 30).

In Morrison's another novel, *Song of Solomon*, "the myth of flying Africans" (Beaulieu 31) depicts the history of African slaves who fled the slave trade by jumping from slave ships during the Middle Passage. The novel begins and ends with a hope for flight which symbolizes the hope of African diaspora in the postcolonial world. Questions about home are also apparent in the novel *Beloved* where the Milkman struggles to explore the family history through folk songs. The narrative-within-narrative which is named as "Sweet Home" addresses "the complexities of the postcolonial figure within the context of home" (Beaulieu 31). Thus, it can be said that the "idea of home for the descendants of African slaves is one where home is and is not Africa, and home is and is not America: "home" is lost and gained, gained and lost" (Beaulieu 31).

The culture of the colonized has been defamed during the

colonial period and the native culture of the nations has been termed as inferior. Hence, the colonies need the colonizer's superior culture and education to be civilized. However, Toni Morrison, along with other postcolonial writers, has reclaimed this second-class status of the colonial nations in the postcolonial world through her works from *The Bluest Eye* to *Paradise* and rejoices the intricacy of Black experiences. Hence, Toni Morrison can be considered a postcolonial critic who depicts the notion of struggle in the postcolonial world.

The use of vision, reimagined relationships and redirected gaze in Toni Morrison's fiction helps in understanding her language and narrative techniques. Morrison's concern for social relationships and her readers who are outside the text as well as the ones who are involved in production and publication of her novels have produced her specific narrative choices. Hence, the philosophical intentions of Morrison shape language and narrative of her novels. American literature, traditionally, considers the readers as White and the Black narrator has always been considered unreliable, which imposes trouble for Black women writers in expressing their own epistemological viewpoint. Morrison uses "particular textual strategies to claim conversational authority and to respond to the needs of the readers. The most significant textual strategies Morrison uses are – extra-representational acts, the disposition of an ideal narrative audience, and recursion" (Ryan 152). Thus, the use of precise semantic and particular narrative techniques by Morrison highlights fictional and non-fictional objectives of African-American literature.

Morrison responds to the needs of the readers while focusing on the "representation, participation and interpretive competence and expresses her commitment to the democracy of social relationships" (Ryan 154). Judylyn Ryan in "Language and Narration in Morrison's Novels" writes:

> Morrison's fiction inscribes enlarged parameters of reader positioning and agency... This involves the deployment of language and narrative techniques that unveil her own authorial presence, and that calls attention to her role in scripting the reader's position so that she or he consciously experiences her/his position as scripted, as part of a collaborative relationship, as an exchange of gazes. (154)

Thus, it can be said that Toni Morrison's novels carve a reader as a co-creator of the text, rather than any consumer or decoder. She also expects that the readers possess certain capabilities and assists them in reclaiming and strengthening these abilities through the use of certain narrative techniques in her fiction.

In conclusion, it can be said that Morrison's writings offer a new model for African American literature by imitating Douglass's notion of ideal narrative spectators as an instrument for accumulating informal authority of the narrator. While Douglass constructed a narrative audience that was in prerequisite of inducement and was persuadable, Morrison has constructed an ideal narrative audience that can be taught and is situated to admit the speaker's awareness, intellect and decent judgments. Morrison has used these strategies to negotiate the task of writing for the privileged readers both racially and culturally, as she writes, "As determined as these Black writers were to persuade the reader of the evil of slavery, they also complimented him by assuming his nobility of heart and his high-mindedness. They tried to summon up his finer nature in order to encourage him to employ it" (Morrison, "The Site of Memory", 6).

Thus, Morrison as a Black feminist, womanist and postcolonial critic gets the opportunity to rebuild her authorial audience as the maturity of audience was not reflected in the nineteenth-century writings because of the common American attitude towards race and Blackness. Here, it can be concluded that in her novels, Toni Morrison divulges the world with such transparency that the readers are encouraged to reconsider their actions and attitudes towards a particular race or class.

## Works Cited

Beaulieu, Elizabeth Ann, Editors. *The Toni Morrison Encyclopedia*. Greenwood Press, 2003.

Stover, Johnnie M. "Approaches to Morrison's Work: Feminist/Black Feminist." *The Toni Morrison Encyclopedia* Eds. Elizabeth Ann Beaulieu. Greenwood Press, 2003, pp. 12-20.

Ivory, James M. "Approaches to Morrison's Work: Postcolonial." *The Toni Morrison Encyclopedia* Eds. Elizabeth Ann Beaulieu. Greenwood Press, 2003, pp. 29-33.

Rosa, Deborah De. "Approaches to Morrison's Work: Womanist." *The Toni Morrison Encyclopedia* Eds. Elizabeth Ann Beaulieu. Greenwood Press, 2003, pp. 39-49.

Collins, Patricia H. "Defining Black Feminist Thought," in *Black Feminist Thought: Knowledge, Consciousness, and the Politics of Empowerment* by Patricia Collins, 1990.

Hooks, Bell. *Talking Back: Thinking Feminist, Thinking Black*. South End Press, 1989.

Ryan, Judylyn S. "Language and Narrative Technique in Toni Morrison's Novels." *The Cambridge Companion to Toni Morrison* Eds. Justine Tally. Cambridge University Press, 2007.

SECTION FOUR

# SUBALTERNISM, REPRODUCTIONS AND EXPERIMENTS

CHAPTER 10

# Reclaiming Oneself

## Subaltern Perspectives in *Beloved*

Sneha Sawai

DEBATES OVER marginalization have always occupied a pivotal place in literary discourses. The contrast between the haves and the have-nots, the privileged and the neglected, the powerful and the distressed have played a crucial role in understanding the complex layers of social reality that gets projected through various forms of literature. A separate branch of critical theory named 'Subaltern Studies' gained prominence in the literary field since 1960s. The word 'Subaltern' was coined by Italian Marxist Antonio Francesco Gramsci and comes from the Latin words 'sub' which means below and 'alternus' which means all others. The term refers to anyone who belongs to a lower rank or has a lower status in society. In critical theory and postcolonial discourse, the term 'Subaltern' refers to people who are marginalized and who are socially, politically, economically and geographically outside hegemonic power structures. Marxist historians who were influenced by Gramsci used the term 'subaltern' to denote the proletariat or the lower class. However, there was a major shift in the application of the term in subsequent years. Various theorists such as Ranajit Guha,

Partha Chatterjee, Homi K Bhabhi, Dipesh Chakrabaty, Galati Speak and Gyanendra Pandey deployed the term for wider meaning and included several subordinate groups (such as people belonging to the lower class, the lower caste or the dalits, peasants, the non-White races, the African Americans, women, children, migrant workers in urban areas and tribal people) who have been denied access to power in the larger fabric of society. The literary movement of the Subaltern Studies aimed at giving voice to the untapped emotions, anguishes and sufferings of the marginalized people and to challenge the larger power hierarchy of the society that oppresses them. Highlighting the complex social web of power within which individual agency of the subalterns gets suppressed, Galati Speak in her famous essay 'Can the Subaltern speak?' declares that the subaltern lack the agency to voice themselves and thereby, highlighted the ambiguity and the social responsibility of the representations made by literary writers that explored the traumatic experiences of the subalterns.

Creating consciousness among the subalterns and to constantly question the dominant ideologies and history was a major preoccupation of the African-American writer Toni Morrison. Her novel *Beloved* (1987) is an excellent example of exploring and addressing the problems of being at the margins. Based on the story of a slave Margaret Garner, who killed her daughter to protect her from the cruel life of slavery (a story that Morrison came across in a newspaper article 'A visit to the Slave Mother Who Killed her Child' published in the American Baptist in 1856 during the course of her editorial work for the Black Book at Random House) Morrison attempted to reconstruct and rewrite Afro-American history from the perspective of the marginalized mother. Through her novel *Beloved*, Morrison explores the debilitating consequences of the social structures of race and gender on African American community and attempts to provide an alternative historiography by not only giving voice to the repressed feelings of the African Americans but also unearthing their suppressed history. Describing her writing as "archaeological explorations", Morrison attempts to create political consciousness among the African Americans by making them aware of the ruthless racist ideologies that robbed them of their individual identity and history leading to 'collective amnesia' among their race.

In order to understand the political significance of *Beloved*, it becomes important for the readers and scholars to study the discourse of history of that time. Set in the Reconstruction Era, the novel looks back to the historical period of slavery, the Atlantic slave trade (when Africans were transported to the New Land) and the 1850s (when the Fugitive slave law was passed). The novel not only attempts to provide alternative history but also questions and interrogates the knowledge circulated by the dominant discourse of history which was essentially Eurocentric. Morrison endeavors to counter the mainstream Eurocentric history by giving voice to the victims. Instead of looking at historical factual details as recorded by the dominant White historians, Morrison looks at history from the emotional view point of the African Americans. Through the use of the stream-of-consciousness narrative technique, Morrison probes into the psyche of the Black characters and attempts to reconstruct history through their fragmented memories and flashbacks. Memories which are considered to be unreliable and inauthentic are given prime importance in the text to recover history which is both personal and national. Unlike slave narratives, the story is not told to us from the perspective and experiences of one character but from various characters belonging to the same community. Through these shifting perspectives of different characters, the author tries to encapsulate the common history of the brutal victimization and oppression of the African Americans not only in the past but also in the present.

Helene Moglen's essay 'Redeeming History: Toni Morrison's Beloved' discusses how the novel explores the racist ideologies that are formed in the society through the binary opposition of the self and the other and how the 'other' serves as an essential instrument in the construction of the self. By giving a psychological insight into her characters, Morrison depicts how the past experiences form an integral part of their personal identity. The Black characters are shown to be struggling to form a new identity even after their emancipation. Paul D, for instance, is unable to get away from his previous identity that was given to him by his master Mr Garner. He insists on calling himself 'Paul D Garner' and struggles with the concept of manhood—"the last of the Sweet Home Men" (7)—that was given to him by his master. The novel therefore, is not just about revising and recovering silenced history through the repressed painful memories of the past but is also about the brutal necessity of the African Americans to establish a new social identity independent of the racist structures prevalent in the society. Through the narrative technique of stream-of-consciousness, Morrison depicts how characters belonging to the three generations (slave trade, the 1850s and the Reconstruction Era) are struggling to deal with their repressed painful memories which results in complete loss and disorientation of the self. The characters are shown to use different strategies to deal with their repressed memories which lead to their alienated or marginalized existence. Baby Suggs, for instance, ponders over and longs for different colors (other than black and white) in order to forget her past. Sethe tries to keep her "past at bay" (51) to survive in the present. Paul D on the other hand, locks his painful memories in a tobacco tin with its "lid rusted shut" which he buries deep in his chest where "a red heart used to be" (86). Having knowledge of the past becomes important even for Denver who belongs to the Reconstruction Era and who has never had a firsthand experience of slavery. She feels anxious to understand herself and the people around her who constantly talk about their past. By depicting characters struggling to deal with their past Morrison emphasizes on the mental conflict that the subaltern face. Even though they were legally free during the Reconstruction Era, they are shown to be victims of their past experiences during slavery which continually haunts them. Confrontation with the past in order to form a new stable self therefore, becomes a very important theme of the text. A confrontation with the past not only allows the characters to move on in future but also empowers them to understand their individual being and associate significant meaning with their self. The ghost Beloved therefore, becomes an important character in the text that is not only a physical manifestation of Sethe's dead daughter but also becomes a symbolic representative of the haunting past both on individual and community levels. She represents the collective memory of 'Sixty Million and More' (epigraph) Africans who died during the Middle Passage which was conveniently overlooked and neglected by the dominant White historians. She represents a whole lineage of "dead and the angry" people who were obliterated by slavery and whose stories were "disremembered and unaccounted for." (323). According to Emma Parker, Beloved's description of her experience in the slave ship indicates that she represents the memory of her African ancestors rather than simply being the ghost of Sethe's dead daughter. Morrison attempts to recreate the horrific brutal experiences and massive deaths of the captured slaves during the Middle Passage from Africa to America through the ghost Beloved that continually haunted and reminded the Black characters of the brutality of the unjust racist structure. Further, we see that it is through the character of Beloved that characters such as Sethe, Paul D, Denver, Stamp Paid, Ella and others are able to confront their past by acknowledging their ancestral history and understanding their individuality. Beloved's provocation to Paul D – "to touch me on the inside part and call me my name" is not only sexual provocation but is also a provocation for confrontation with his past (which is similar to the brutal inhuman experiences of his ancestors) that Beloved embodies in flesh and blood. It is only through his sexual encounter with Beloved that Paul D is able to confront his repressed pain and suffering and is able to restore his "red heart" by acknowledging his feelings and vulnerabilities. Similarly, the presence of Beloved makes other characters reflect upon their past to be able to form a new self. It is only through this confrontation that characters are able to reclaim their identity and their cultural heritage. Beloved therefore acts as a catalyst for social and cultural assertion. In his discussion of W.E.B. Du Bois's *The Souls of Black Folk*

(1903) Arnold Rampersad describes this recovery of history as both national and personal necessity:

> [Du Bois's] point of view is clear. Admitting and exploring the reality of slavery is necessarily painful for a Black American, but only by doing so can he/she begin to understand himself or herself and American and Afro-American culture in general. The normal price of the evasion of the fact of slavery is intellectual and spiritual death. Only by grappling with the meaning and legacy of slavery can the imagination, recognizing finally the temporality of the institution begin to transcend it (395).

Morrison not only projects the realistic and horrifying picture of the oppression that the African Americans suffered during slavery when "men and women were moved around like checkers" (27) but also depicts the atrocities and challenges faced by them as marginalized people in contemporary America where they are "free". Through the depiction of brutality perpetrated by the Whites and the racial discrimination prevalent in the society, Morrison questions the functioning of the racist stereotypes and questions the notion of freedom granted by America.

Morrison condemns not only the institution of slavery but also the educational institution of America that propagated racist ideologies through the character of the Schoolteacher. According to Krumholz, Schoolteacher's pedagogical and interpretive educational methods are morally bereft as they adopt a 'Manichean opposition'—"put her [Sethe] human characteristics on the left, her animal ones on the right." (193). Using the framework provided by the new historicists and cultural materialists one can say that Morrison demonstrates how hegemonic discourses, definitions and historical methods are constructed in a society. They are neither arbitrary nor objective instead they become instrumental in propagating unjust racial hierarchy. Morrison forces the readers to question the authority of the hegemonic discourses which forms the basis of a racist society through Sixo who exemplifies how access to basic human rights to voice or express himself has been denied to him. When he tries to defend himself from the charge of theft the Schoolteacher beats him up to demonstrate his power and to show that African Americans have a marginalized existence where they do not have the agency to speak or question the authority and that definition of power belonged to the powerful 'definers' i.e., the Whites and not the 'defined'.

Paul D's refusal to accept that the picture in the newspaper clipping was that of Sethe is a reflection on the kind of historical documents that were circulated. It was the hegemonic group who decided what would "qualify" as important news and supervised the information recorded in historical documents. Through the use of the newspaper clipping Morrison questions the representation of the marginalized African Americans in the 'official' historical documents where their perspective was not taken into consideration by the hegemonic class. The authenticity of the "official" version of history is further questioned by the author when she attempts to provide three different versions of Sethe's act of killing Beloved. According to the White Schoolteacher Sethe's act of killing her daughter was a "testimony to the results of a little so-called freedom imposed on people who needed every care and guidance in the world to keep them from the cannibal life they preferred."

Her act of killing her daughter was seen as a reinforcement of the racist stereotypes by the Schoolteacher which helps him validate his power and authority. For Stamp Paid however Sethe's act was a "rough response to the Fugitive Bill" (171) which resulted due to the "meanness" (185) of the community who did not warn her about the schoolteacher. But for Sethe, killing of Beloved was a way to "put my babies where they'd be safe." (193) Having experienced the atrocities of slavery Sethe believed that the only way to secure safety for her kids was by putting them to death. It throws light on the psychological impact of the brutal life of slavery which robs them of their identity. By providing alternate versions of the same event, Morrison questions the 'official' historical facts which were represented in the newspaper article on Margaret Garner and provides insight into subaltern reality which gets neglected and distorted by the hegemonic group.

The historical and pedagogical practices prevalent in the US are further critiqued by the use of the African-American oral and literary tradition. Morrison incorporates the African conventions of storytelling in her narrative to deconstruct the 'official' version of history. The story of Sethe is narrated by various characters each adding new information through their fragmented memories. The story is repeated and remembered through the consciousness of various characters providing a multiplicity of perspectives and historical positions. This kind of non-linear and fragmented recounting of the past challenges the notions of objectivity in the creation of history. The oral tradition of storytelling and singing songs becomes an important mode of reconstructing the past and resistance in Beloved.

Furthermore, Morrison's *Beloved* not only looks at the racist aspect of history but also depicts the sexist attitudes prevalent not just outside the Black community but amply present within the community. By giving voice to African American women who are doubly marginalized (on the basis of their gender and their race) Morrison critiques the patriarchal structure of the society that oppresses women and limits their possibilities. In her endeavor to reclaim cultural history and identity Morrison also gives expression to the doubly marginalized experiences that get overlooked and neglected in the larger rubrics of race battle. Black women not only face oppression at the hands of the Whites but also from Black men of their own community. This gender disparity is clearly depicted in the relationship between Paul D and Sethe. Paul D is introduced by Morrison as "the last of Sweet Home Men" (7) who becomes the epitome of self-contained masculinity. He, like all other 'Sweet Home men' is encouraged by Garner's illusion to inherit masculine attitude according to the White patriarchal standards. However, with the arrival of the Schoolteacher he realizes that they were 'men' only at Sweet Home plantation under the supervision of Mr Garner. This shatters Paul D in the wake of the realization of the reality of slavery and results in his identity crisis. Even though he feels proud of Sethe for being able to successfully run away from the plantation, he feels the need to mark over her and take charge of the house. For him the idea of a normal family centers around a man. In order to validate and reestablish his identity (which is essentially based on the patriarchal understanding of masculinity) which gets challenged through the manipulation of Beloved, he feels the need to impregnate Sethe. This is a clear indication of the patriarchal hierarchy that existed within the community.

Morrison also explores the complexity of the Black womens' experiences through her female characters. The experiences of the Black female are shown to be very different from that of their male counterpart. One of the most important themes of the text is of motherhood and rape. Morrison depicts how slavery destroyed not only families but also individual beings. Throughout the novel Baby Suggs laments about not been able to keep her children with her - "Not a house in the country ain't packed to its rafters with some negro's grief...You[Sethe] lucky. You got three left. Three pulling at your skirts and just one raising hell from the other side. Be thankful, why don't you. I had eight. Every one of them gone away from me. Four taken, four chased...Eight children and that's all I remember." (6) Like Baby Suggs's fading memory of her children, Sethe too has a very faint memory of her mother. She recounts how she never got the opportunity to spend time with her mother. All she remembers is the mark of a cross and a circle that was branded on her mother's body with which she associates her mother. The basic right of the child to be nursed by its mother was also denied to her. "By the time I woke up in the morning, she was in line. If the moon was bright they worked by its light. Sunday she slept like a stick... Then she went back in rice and I sucked from another woman whose job it was... She didn't even sleep in the same cabin most nights I remember." (72) What we get to see is objectification of slave mothers who were classified as "breeders" (as pointed by J. Brooks Bouson) as opposed to mothers whose children could be bought and sold.

The harrowing experiences of slavery scarred African American women both mentally and physically robbing them of their idea of self. All female characters are shown to be dealing with the trauma of rape. Sethe's repetitive emphasis on her stolen milk signifies the psychological impact of rape that justifies her act of killing her daughter. The novel is not just about a single mother Sethe who killed her daughter to save her from slavery instead it mirrors the acts or crimes of the thirty women who gathered near Sethe's house to exorcise the ghost. Like Sethe, Sethe's mother and Ella could not fulfill their duty of being a mother as in an act of defiance they refused to nurse their babies begotten from rape. It is their shared guilt that makes all thirty women gather at the end of the novel to help Sethe and to confront their forgotten past. The horror of rape is also portrayed through Beloved's interior monologue where she describes the experiences of the Middle Passage during the Atlantic Slave Trade. Through the character of Beloved, Morrison gives voice to the horrific experiences of Black women during the Middle Passage where women were repeatedly raped and exploited by the White crew members. Recounting the horrific experiences Beloved depicts the immense fear that harbored within young girls who were scared of the 'ghosts without skin' i.e. White men. Morrison's Beloved therefore, provides a saga of Black women's suffering and their subaltern experiences.

The novel is also replete with strong female characters who try to resist and challenge patriarchal power. Baby Suggs becomes an important female character who questions the power hierarchy by choosing a name for herself. She refuses to call herself Jenny which was a name given to her by her master. She asserts her individuality by taking up a name that her husband used to call her after getting her freedom. She also becomes a spiritual leader for her community "an unchurched preacher" (102) and dismantles the notion of spirituality and slavery propagated by the Church. She urges her community members – men, women and children to "reclaim their body." Through the character of Baby Suggs, Morrison urges both Black men and women to reclaim and "prize" their bodies, their wounds and their past.

She did not tell them to clean up their lives or to go and sin no more. She did not tell them they were blessed of the earth, its inheriting meek or its glorybound pure. She told them that the only grace they could have was the grace they could imagine… 'Here,' she said, 'in this here place, we flesh: flesh that weeps, laughs; flesh that dances on bare feet in grass. Love it. Love it hard.' (103)

Morrison uses her writing to reclaim the history of the Black women and urges women to reclaim their bodies and their past. By discussing the experiences of the African American mothers Morrison constructs a new narrative of Black history. She rejected the formulation of a homogeneous identity of the African Americans and emphasized on the differences prevalent within the Black society. The novel not only subverts the negative stereotypes constructed by the White writings that were dominant but also counters the stereotypes promulgated by the Black men. It established a new identity for Black women and resisted the male domination prevalent in the society.

Morrison's *Beloved*, therefore, deconstructs the traditional discourse of history and critiques the larger power structures prevalent in the society by giving voice to the African Americans.

## Works Cited

Barnett, Pamela E. "Figurations of Rape and the Supernatural in Beloved." *PMLA*, vol. 112.

States of America: Modern Language Association, 1997. JSTOR. Web. 10 December 2018.

Bloom, Harold. Toni Morrison's *Beloved.* United States of America: Chelsea House Publishers, 2004.

Harris, Trudier. "Escaping Slavery but Not Its Images." *Toni Morrison: Critical Perspectives Past and Present.* New York: Amistad Press, 1993.

Krumholz, Linda. "The Ghosts of Slavery: Historical Recovery in Toni Morrison's Beloved." *African American Review*, Vol. 26, Indiana: Indiana State University, 1992. JSTOR. Web. 8 December 2018.

Moglen, Helene. "Redeeming History: Toni Morrison's Beloved." *Cultural Critique* (No.24) Minnesota: University of Minnesota Press, 1993. JSTOR. Web. 8 December 2018.

Morrison, Toni. *Beloved.* UK: Vintage, 2005.

Pal, Sunanda. "From Periphery to Centre: Toni Morrison's Self Affirming Fiction." *Economic and Political Weekly*, Vol. 29. India: *Economic and Political Weekly*, 1994. JSTOR. Web. 9 December 2018.

CHAPTER 11

# Reproduction of Sexual Power Politics

## A Critique of *Sula*

Dipankar Parui

SEXUALITY IS an integral branch of the biological system of any living being. Various studies have shown that the manifestations of sexuality are diverse in relation to biology and social construct. Sexual conduct and behaviour may be witnessed as the effect of how cultural and societal upbringing shape an individual amid his social existence. Generally, we are guided and influenced by the tradition and the etiquette of the society we live in. The standard of gender construction is inherited by the environment and our ancestors. But for the last few centuries, the major gender principle reveals a kind of misbalanced power between the opposite sexes and it is submerged into the human psyche. Of late, the intricacy and mystery of human sexuality have become a popular area of study in literature. The theme of sexuality has all the time been utilized to lure readers by inciting feelings of love, libido and oppression. This article primarily focuses on one of the most prolific and talented Afro-American novelists Toni Morrison's novel *Sula* (1973) with the aim to unearth the relationship between gender and sexual politics.

Nobel Laureate, Toni Morrison has been considered one of the most creative and gifted writers of the 20th and 21st centuries who achieved several accolades for her literary outputs. She was deeply engaged with the issues of race, gender, love, sexuality and oppression. Toni Morrison's works have been described as "amazingly high" which mingle the objectives of women's liberation and Black Freedom Movement. All the fictions produced by her with these aims are irretrievably and unquestionably Black. She expresses with a keen sense of sadness or regret what it looks to be Black and female as well. To be Black and female is to experience double handicaps of ethnic bigotry and distinct gender bias. Being female, they were the sufferers of sexual violence at the hands of White patriarchs as well as the African Americans and by being black, these African women suffered from racial discrimination. The Whites strained them to live on scanty resources as they were former slaves. So, it can be deciphered that African American Women in America were under triple jeopardy-racism, sexism and classism.

It is presumed that every society has an order and that is created by the people, the inhabitants of the generations. Morrison's novels are replete with the delineation of a kind of misbalanced power between the opposite sexes in the societal milieu and consequently this imbalance is manifested through the psychological conflicts of the characters. In all her fictions, gender has been the leading theme and moulds the conflicts of the characters. Sexuality is the ground upon which these divergences are raised. Morrison shows diverse facets of sexuality to expose the development of the theme of gender role with the society and the impact of the societal ambience over the psyche, mental states, feelings and deeds of the characters. Morrison had a point that to avoid a sick society we need to discard a sick sexuality. She shows the sexual behaviour of her characters and the misbalance amid the opposite genders that may lead to divergences between individuals and non-performing relationships among them.

Toni Morrison in her novel *Sula*, (1973) mainly delineates two propositions, which are the consequences of racial discrimination on the construction of African American identity and the impact of sexism on Black feminine identity. She tries to concentrate on the individual African American woman fighting to achieve selfhood as well as freedom as found similarly in *Meridian* by Alice Walker published in 1976. Both the novelists speak of a similar truth out of "collective consciousness" to construct feminine identity as "Spiritual sisters". In *Sula* we have noticed that the men discard their women and are characterised as immature, unreliable, dishonest and unnamed as we found in the names of Green, BoyBoy, Deweys etc. On the other hand, the women are endowed with empowering names with enough physical, emotional and financial support.

We get all the feminine characters in Morrison's *Sula* but the story is the development of the main protagonist Sula from her adolescence when she was an isolated small girl to her demise when she became the object of disgust due to her licentious nature. Even she has become the object of superstition as she lives at the segregated part of the town. The novel is centered around the camaraderie of Sula Peace and Nel Wright, the two dark complexioned girls on a milieu of an imaginary African American neighbourhood Bottom, on the hill above the fictional town of Medallion, Ohio. They both grow up with no father figure. They are reared in this tiny, closely knit, insular African American community of Medallion. Here the lives of the women are supposed to be more submissive, righteous, home bound, church going whereas the men are supposed to be emotionally reserved and source of income generators as well as bread earners. The Bottom neighbourhood has been more than a mere backdrop of the fiction and the town itself is the character in its own way. Rubenstein has rightly pointed out, "the community of the Bottom.........is not only a place but a presence; a kind of collective conscience that arbitrates the social and moral norms of its members" (148). This fictional town is the basis for revolt and exploration which Sula represents. Morrison has presented the character of Shadrack in chapter labelled with year *1919* and then Nel labelled with year *1920*, after that in *1922*, the character of Sula is introduced. This is how Morrison opens the environment in which Sula grows up and ultimately it shapes her character, personality and sexuality.

Sula's grandmother Eva commits an awful act of deserting her children by keeping them under a fellow citizen of the neighbourhood only to return back after a year depending on crutches as she had her one leg amputated. Eva had a terrible plan of claiming the indemnity price from the railways after her self-willed accident. She did it to nourish the poverty-stricken family with no food and money to support the children (31). Trudier Harris views this sacrifice of her leg as an act of self-conservation through which she recuperates her freedom and proves herself to the outside, the moral norms of the society, "her freedom, somehow tied to the loss of her leg and gives her the ability to love, hate, create, conquer and kill, with responsibility and accountability only to herself" (73).

> It was man love that Eva bequeathed to her daughters. Probably people said, there were no men in the house, no men to run it........... The Peace women simply loved maleness, for its own sake (41).

Besides bestowing this type of man-love to her daughters, she also hands down "a capacity for emotional distance that allows for the creation of a female self" (Gillespie and Kubitschek 76). Eva and Hannah both have self-governing abilities and both are physically alluring to the men folk and their moderately unprejudiced, broad-minded heterosexual relationship is significant to the future behaviour of sexuality in Sula. Deborah E. McDowell declares, "Sula's female heritage is an unbroken line of 'man-loving' woman who exist as sexually desirable subjects rather than as objects of male desire" (82). According to Rubenstein, Sula has got the legacy of sensual debauchery from her mother. Sula was reared amid the environment of licentiousness which paved the way for her distress and devastation with the affairs with men folk. After becoming intimate friends, Sula and Nel, both were almost inseparable but obviously basic differences remain like the process of upbringing, their mother's attitude and their different home environment. The development of womanhood of Nel and Sula, the two African American women, serves to analyse the remarkable disagreement of life. They seem to be the two sides of the same coin. Morrison tells, "Their friendship was so close, they themselves had difficulty distinguishing one's thoughts from the other's" (83). When Sula comes back to

Bottom, Nel welcomes the return of her friend as 'getting an eye back' and a conversation with her is forever 'a conversation with herself'.

Nel is born into a middle-class family. She is the child who grows up in a stable home with a mother knee deep in social traditions and conventions. Helene, Nel's mom has performed almost all that she could do to aloof herself from the prostitute-mother of her living in New Orleans. "Helene projects and channels the fear of her own mother's 'outlaw' sexuality into controlling repression of Nel's sexuality" (Demetrakopoulos 53). The Peace family is just the other way around. Sula Peace's family lives in 'a woolly house' (29) which itself is dirty, dingy and unorganized. Eva, her grandmother and Hannah, her mom, both stay with Sula and are considered in the town as eccentric and loose though Hannah is loved by all the men folk and Eva is respected by all women. Nel loves to visit Sula's house which lacks tidiness and order and may be termed as "masculine" with a touch of an orthodox bachelor's way of lodging and living. Sula sometimes becomes disobedient and scoffs at Nel's harshly neat and orderly home, though, Sula "loved it and would sit on the red velvet sofa for ten to twenty minutes at a time-still as dawn" (29). Her rearing is rather dissimilar and in the pandemonium of a family of strange and odd women; she has also given a fight back to achieve a sense of her own individualism akin to that of Nel.

Sula's mother fails to provide her that much comfort and nurturing which she requires and alternatively she finds and fulfils that lack in her friendship with Nel. They become fiercely attached to each other in adolescent friendship which fosters both the pubescent girls by replenishing the severe dearth of natural bondage between mother and daughter. Sula's consideration about herself and her friend runs identical; but Nel is much more conscious about the limits and margins in a decisive moment. Morrison has given descriptions of physical and sensual experiences of these pubescent girls who are surprisingly conscious of their sexuality with flesh tightening and shaking. At the same moment they are delighted and uneasy with their tiny breasts protruding. These two adolescent girls were so close to each other that without uttering any words, they can understand what the other is thinking or what the 'game' is about. Morrison further uses languages like 'tightened and shivered', 'stripped', 'a smooth creamy innocence', 'undressed', 'poked' and 'rhythmically and intense' which carry a potency of sensual implications. They cease to play their 'grass-play' and appear to be dismayed with their beings. Gillespie and Kubitschek assert, "Sula's preservation of herself allows Nel to limn boundaries between herself and her mother; in turn, Nel's attention to details of connection and her calm consistently allow Sula's rigid boundaries to become more fluid" (41). Sula gets calm and peace by staying in and around Nel and her mom. Nel also learns the meaning of recognition and satisfaction within the home of Sula. Nel gives Sula vitality, vigour and dependability and in return she provides Nel, attachment and emotion (53). Two girls enjoy one another's company throughout, until Nel marries Jude. Sula takes a 'clean break' by taking leave from Nel's community when she gets married.

Some critics have labelled the relationship between Sula and Nel as homoerotic. Barbara Smith rightly observes, "Despite the apparent heterosexuality of the female characters, I discovered in re-reading *Sula* that it works as a lesbian novel not only because of the passionate friendship between Sula and Nel, but because of Morrison's consistently critical stance towards the heterosexual institution of male-female relationships, marriage and family" (Smith 165).

Sexuality has been the predominating issue in Sula's friendship with Nel. According to Agnes Suranyi, it is evident that the basic theme of the fiction is the bonding of African American women which has strong lesbian connotations. Adrienne Rich also asserts, "The Girl and Sula are both novels which reveal the lesbian continuum in contrast to the shallow or sensational 'lesbian scenes' in recent commercial fiction. Each shows us woman-identification untarnished....... by romanticism" (656). Alisha R. Coleman mentions Smith's misreading of the "emotional intimacy" between these two adolescent girls. Coleman emphasizes that in this narrative Sula and Nel turn it into a feminist fiction where these two girls 'complete' and 'complement' each other, generating 'two halves of a personality that combine to form a whole psyche" (151). The two adolescent girls' bond makes a 'safe harbour for each other's company' where they can 'afford to abandon the ways of other people and concentrate on their own perceptions of things' (55). In an interview with Claudia Tate, Morrison said, "Nobody ever talked about friendship between women unless it was homosexual and there is no homosexuality in *Sula.* Relationships between women were always written about as though they were subordinate to some other roles they play. This is not true of men" (157). Morrison is not interested and agrees to subscribe the view of a queer reading of *Sula* but delineates a very strong bonding of hearts between these two female characters without being involved in gross carnal sensuality.

On the day of Nel's marriage, Sula leaves the town with a smile and returns back there after ten long years. She was bored during her days of college and during the time of her travel. It was her sexuality which holds only ennui and depression. Instead of manifesting human connection and mystic insight, she is involved in gross physical intercourse and it increases her loneliness and despair. On the other hand, Nel has turned into a very traditional, straightforward voice of a woman with its value of caring and protecting others, the training she got from her family. But Sula, in contrast, is self centered, only concerned with herself and with her own responsibilities. Sexuality has become an issue in the friendship of Sula with Nel. This deep bonding of friendship is devastated and ruined by Sula at the end when she shares bed with Nel's husband. In this regard, Morrison writes:

> ......Nel waited. Waited for the oldest cry. A scream not for others, not in sympathy for a burnt child or a dead father, but a deeply personal cry for one's own pain. A loud strident: "Why me?" she waited. (*Sula* 108)

As a consequence, Nel undergoes a trauma of double deprivation by losing both her friend as well as husband, ".... that was too much. To lose Jude and not have Sula to talk to about it because it was Sula that he had left her for" (110). It was an unfathomable wound that Sula inflicts upon Nel who considers sexual intimacy as something sacred in a post-marriage relationship. She thinks that she has been deprived of both love and sex and definitely loses a true bonding and friendship with Sula. Moreover, she reaches the nadir of despair and loneliness. Christian perfectly points out that of psychological bearing since childhood, as Sula and Nel shared everything from then, Sula tries to get more intimate with Nel by sharing Nel's husband. This is because of Sula's sexually liberated psyche. Contrary to that, "Nel's sexuality is not expressed in itself and for her own pleasure, but rather, for the pleasure of her husband and in obedience to a system of ethical judgement and moral virtue.......because Nel's sexuality is harassed to and only enacted with the institutions that sanction sexuality for women-marriage and family-she does not own it" (McDowell 82). With this sexual promiscuity Sula distances herself from the conventional people of the town Bottom. Nel discards her own emotions which can be socially expected and receives Sula's hatred and disgust at the dishonesty she plays with. Nel adheres to the commune to watch Sula as a 'pariah' (122), a 'selfish' and Sula judges her as 'one of them....one of the spiders'. Nel as well as the entire Bottom's denunciation of Sula, as a severe experimenter of life, is a microcosmic reflection of the rejection of the community.

When the news spreads over Bottom about the frivolous, licentious involvement of Sula, the entire community recognizes her as "guilty of doing the unforgiveable thing-the thing for which there was no understanding, no excuse, no compassion" (96). Sula's position as a man-less woman and children is being rejected in Bottom as the people of Bottom think that children are a part of the order of things though Sula does not care at all and is 'dangerously free'. To her only her freedom matters. When asked by Eva, "when you gone to get married? You need to have some babies. It'll settle you down" (92), Sula replies, "I don't want to make somebody else. I want to make myself" (92). "Her own business- the business of being, of living-is not dictated by family and community" (Galehouse 352). Her shameless sexuality and denying of conventional womanhood and motherhood may fetch her on the threshold of feminist heroine but from the middle-class perspective, it gets more complicated with the African American identity perspective. Thus, in *Sula* 'gender identity is also race-inflected' (Bouson 47). Sula ".......rebels against the role she is assigned to take within the Black community. Consequently, she becomes a transgressor and an outlaw" (Suranyi 20). Sula's heroic search for White men falls outside the moral policy of the society. Even her meeting with copious lovers exemplifies how her sexuality is crippled, paralyzed and disappointed.

In this novel, Morrison's main eloquent proclamation about the deprivation of a woman that appears earlier in a paragraph that surfaces after the first encounter of them: "Because each had discovered years before they were neither White nor male, and that all freedom and triumph was forbidden to them, they had set about creating something else to be" (52). Both the teenagers receive love, uniqueness and security which are robbed from them at their respective homes from each other. They jointly set foot into pubescence, they unearth and recognize males, and they become conscious of their sexual orientation and desirability.

> Their friendship was as intense as it was sudden. They found relief in each other's personality. Although both were unshaped, formless things, Nel seemed stronger and more consistent than Sula who could hardly be counted on to sustain any emotion for more than three minutes (53).

'Apart from being a self-centered iconoclast rejecting the maternal with an ardent view of sexual independency, Sula also commits another unpardonable felony upon her grandmother by putting her in the home of an old and aged folk, her refusal to mother the mother' (Stepto 16). She refuses to accept the conventional ordering principles of the society like marriage, children, grandparental care, sexual customs—this is an automatic response of rebellion on her part.

Justine Tally rightly says, "As with most great authors, Morrison may be talking about the past, but she is speaking to the present" (3). Morrison in this novel, *Sula* critically unearths every individual as well as entire families that become a victim of the gender codes and oppressive sexual behaviour. Even the story of the Peace family is looked upon in a repugnant way by the outsiders of the community due to their promiscuous attitude and lifestyle. Morrison emphatically deconstructs the stereotypical portraits of these women as bold and beautiful to liberate them from the shackles of oppression and restraints of the sexist and the male dominating societies.

According to Mc Bride, "If any one theme might be said to characterize the primary intellectual commitment of Toni Morrison's work, even across genres of fiction and non-fiction, it would be the pursuit of freedom" (166). With the narrative of the novels, she channelizes the psyches of the readers towards the detrimental as well as harmful behavioural codes of specifically those that appear to encompass the modern society, not only confined to Afro-American communities. Through these narratives, Morrison has aims to instruct the readers on how to treat our children as they are the imprints of the manner, behaviour, guidance and love we provide to all of them is pivotal as it determines their mental and psychological health.

## Works Cited

Bouson, J. Brooks. *Quiet as It's Kept: Shame, Trauma and Race in the Novels of Toni Morrison.* States University of New York Press, 2000.

Christian, Barbara. *Black Women Novelists: The Development of a* Tradition, 1892-1976. Greenwood Press, 1980.

Coleman, Alisha R. "One and One Makes One: A Metacritical and Psychoanalytic reading of Friendship in Toni Morrison's Sula." *CLA Journal*, vol. 37, 1993, pp. 145-155.

Demetrakopoulos, Stephanie A. "Sula and the Primacy of Woman-to-Woman Bonds". *New Dimensions of Spirituality: A Biracial and Bicultural Reading of the Novels of Toni Morrison.* Ed. Karla F. C. Holloway and Stephanie A Demetrakopoulos. Greenwood Press, 1987, pp. 51-66.

Galehouse, Maggie. "New World Women: Toni Morrison's Sula." *PLL*, 1999, pp. 339-62.

Gillespie, Diane and Missy Dehn Kubitschek. "Who cares? Women-centered Psychology in *Sula.*" *Understanding Toni Morrison's Beloved and Sula: Selected Essays and Criticisms of the Works by the Nobel Prize-winning Author.* Eds. Solomon O. Iyasere & Marla W. Iyasere. Whitston, 2000, pp. 19-48.

Harris, Trudier. *Fiction and Folklore: The Novels of Toni Morrison.* University of Tennessee Press, 1991.

McBride, Dwight. "Morrison, Intellectual." *The Cambridge Companion to Toni Morrison*. Ed. Justine Tally, Cambridge University Press, 2007, pp. 162-174.

McDowell, Deborah E. "'The Self and the Other': Reading Toni Morrison's *Sula* and the Black Female Text." *Critical Essays on Tonni Morrison*. Ed. Nellie Y. McKay. G K Hall & Co., 1988, pp. 77-90.

Morrison, Tony. *Sula*. New York: Penguin Books, 1982.

Rich, Adrienne. "Contemporary Heterosexuality and Lesbian Existence." *Signs: Journal of Women in Culture and Society* 5, 1980, pp. 631-60.

Rubenstein, Roberta. "Pariahs and Community." *Toni Morrison: Critical Perspectives Past and Present*. Eds. Henry Louis Gates Jr. And K. A. Appiah. New York: Amistad, Inc., 1993, pp. 126-58.

Smith, Barbara. *Towards a Black Feminist Criticism*. Out & Out Books, 1982.

Stepto, Robert. Intimate Things in Place: A Conversation with Toni Morrison." *Chants of Saints*. University of Illinois Press, 1979.

Suranyi, Agnes. "*The Bluest Eye* and *Sula*: Black Female Experience from Childhood to Womanhood." *The Cambridge Companion to Toni Morrison*. Ed. Justine Tally. Cambridge University Press, 2007, pp. 11-25.

Tally, Justine, Ed. *The Cambridge Companion to Toni Morrison*. Cambridge University Press, 2007.

CHAPTER 12

# *Sula*: First Experiment with Magic Realism

Anuradha Bhattacharyya

ONCE ONE'S identity is fixed as a woman, as an African American woman and perhaps as some of the other matters associated with being a African American American, who is marginalized, ostracized or in any other way not mainstream, not upper class or not the dominant race, there is no way one can ask the readers to review her work from any other angle. Her identity is so fused with the written word that the reader inadvertently labels one as Black Feminist.

Yet in *Sula*, Morrison's first attempt at magic realism, more than the identity of the two girls as African American, the story of three generations is evident from the very start. Most of the features of magic realism are identifiable in *Sula*. It is very painful for a twenty first century researcher to notice that this structural feature of the art work in *Sula* has been completely overlooked by the then reviewers of the novel. It may be a happy thing that the book has been appreciated for its feminist approach or for highlighting the African American American community for their generosity, simple mindedness and also their hardships, that these have been treated as more interesting observations about the book but it practically classifies Morrison as a type of writer, definitely separate from the mainstream.

In Morrison's Foreword to the 2004 Vintage eBook of *Sula*, she writes, "politics—all politics—is agenda and therefore its presence taints aesthetic production" (XI). Morrison answers the critics of African American writers with the following words in the 2004 Foreword of the Vintage Classics, "Whether they were wholly uninterested in politics of any sort, or whether they were politically inclined, aware, or aggressive, the fact of their race or the race of their characters doomed them to a "political-only" analysis of their worth" (XI). In this essay, I have made an attempt to explore the artistry in Morrison.

*Sula* begins during the end of the First World War and ends in the year 1965, when the Voting Rights Act for the Black Americans was passed. Between 1850, The Fugitive Slave Act and 1965, tucked up in the hills above Medallion lived a African American community which was free. It was established by the slave who pleased his master by performing a difficult task and in reward got a 'share' of the latter's land and freedom. In true magic realist mode, in line with any of the Latin American authors, Spanish, Germans and Italians who have attempted magic realism, the history and destiny of a settlement is traced from its beginning to the end. The first paragraph foreshadows the end in bulldozing the settlement and turning the land flat into a golf course. As the beginning reads:

> In that place, where they tore the nightshade and blackberry patches from their roots to make room for the Medallion City Golf Course, there was once a neighborhood. It stood in the hills above the valley town of Medallion and spread all the way to the river. It

> is called the suburbs now, but when Black people lived there it was called the Bottom. (Morrison, Sula 3)

Immediately after the hint of its imminent destruction, comes a summary of the whole story that involves two central characters whose actions are intertwined with the destiny of the hill town, Bottom with all its ironical implications. The author then plunges into a detailed narrative about its establishment which illustrates the simplemindedness of the African American Slave. It is up to the reader what part of the narrative draws most attention. It is the reader's privilege to choose whether to call it a commentary on the simplicity of the African Americans or on the hypocrisy of the White farmer. Similarly, it is up to the reader to delve into the life of the girls or on the fate of the community. Not only that, a reader has to look at its aesthetics, as Morrison herself points out in her Foreword to the novel in 2004.

The connections drawn with international events such as the First World War, the Second World War, the construction of the tunnel, previously a bridge and also the gradual spread of the African Americans across the length and breadth of America as free citizens is yet another feature of magic realism. Morrison's novel of 1973 is an early instance of the genre and has been followed by *Beloved,* 1987 in which she adopts the form with greater determination.

*Sula* is a comparatively short piece of fiction, roughly fifty thousand words in length. It follows a well-planned pattern that almost verges on cinematic techniques. Although Morrison tells the tale year wise, her narration concentrates on one vital incident of the year. In this, the superimposition of a chain of events in 1937 which are not detailed is significant. Probably giving all those details would have verged on melodrama. In one instant the yellow and blue striped tie symbolically transports time. From Sula's first day at Nel's household to the discovery of Jude's infidelity and then departure to Nel's weeping over it, the narrative is cinematographic and compresses the whole episode, as vital as it still remains, into a nutshell.

> He left his tie. The one with the scriggly yellow lines running lopsided across the dark-blue field. It hung over the top of the closet door pointing steadily downward while it waited with every confidence for Jude to return.
> Could he be gone if his tie is still here? (Morrison, Sula 103)

Throughout the introduction about Sula's return to Bottom as a liberated, slim and attractive African American woman, ten years after her best friend married, the emphasis is on the life of the settlement. In ten years, whatever Sula did in Nashville, Detroit, New Orleans, New York, Philadelphia, Macon and San Diego (119), nothing is told to us. The narrative does not pursue anyone who goes out of the town. Jude goes to Detroit, Ajax leaves for Detroit, numerous residents go down into the valley for work in the day time but none of their activities are recorded in this text. What we see in one of the earliest magic realist novels is also seen here. Individual actions are made responsible for the destruction of the community.

Not just that, one central family is most actively involved in the progress of the community. The history of that family is a typical cell in the tissue of the entire community. More than anything else, the individual's love of the hometown is supreme. Those who leave for good, never even belonged to the place. Others go away only to be magnetically driven back home. Shadrock returns to his window and his river. Sula returns because she is bored of other places.

Although Shadrock holds up the story in a frame, beginning with the local declaration of the National Suicide Day and ending with the suicide of a sufficient number of residents in the tunnel, he remains on the outskirts of the activities of the town. He sells fish for a living. He interacts with the residents only to sell his fish on Tuesdays and Fridays. He has no attachment towards women. The other townsfolk are surreptitious lovers, blatantly eve-teasers or householders. There are a few who do abandon their family and go away but they do not mark any turning point in the lives of the people in general. But Shadrock's actions have an impact.

> Everybody, Dessie, Tar Baby, Patsy, Mr Buckland Reed, Teapot's Mamma, Valentine, the Deweys, Mrs Jackson, Irene, the proprietor of the Palace of Cosmetology, Reba, the Herrod brothers and flocks of teenagers got into the mood and, laughing, dancing, calling to one another, formed a pied piper's band behind Shadrack. (Morrison, Sula 158)

The novel revolves around the sentiments of Nel. She is the true protagonist, stronger and saner than Sula. She is also the centre of Sula's attention as girls. She is the only one who misses Sula till the end. Nel is introduced first and it is Nel who survives in the end. Sula comes like a breeze in her life at the age of twelve. The author has expressed female bonding in adolescence. It is common in women. It is broken only because of one woman's marriage. Marriage is a duty that removes women from the fun and carefree life of being girls. Nel is married when she is seventeen. In ten years gives birth to three children. It is only after Sula meets her that Nel finds back her carefree laughter.

> Damp-faced, Nel stepped back into the kitchen. She felt new, soft and new. It had been the longest time since she had had a rib-scraping laugh. She had forgotten how deep and down it could be. So different from the miscellaneous giggles and smiles she had learned to be content with these past few years. (Morrison, Sula 97)

At the end of the novel an older Nel visits Sula's grandmother in the old age home. There, the grandmother confuses her with Sula saying they were both the same. It is Nel who goes to the cemetery and weeps at the end of the novel. The intervention of the male partner is almost blamed for the disruption in the life of the two girls. This seals the theme of the book as feminist. It has also been studied as a queer text by Adrianne Rich.

Eva, Sula's grandmother had built a house in Bottom which grows bigger with time. It is about a hundred years old. It is inhabited by many people. Morrison's focus on this house is crucial to the narrative of the text. Eva is the matriarch. She presides over the fates of all the residents of the house. She takes tough decisions. She lives for the longest period. She knows everything about everybody. People feel the strength of her character. She can shelter others and also kill if necessary.

> The creator and sovereign of this enormous house with the four sickle-pear trees in the front yard and the single elm in the back yard was Eva Peace, who sat in a wagon on the third floor directing the lives of her children,

friends, strays, and a constant stream of boarders. (Morrison, Sula 29)

Other than the matriarch, the house and the hundred years, one more magic realist feature of the novel is the symbolism of the robins. It is called the plague of the robins. The advent of the robins in large numbers is associated with the beginning of the destruction of the town. The shit and the dead bodies of the robins at doorsteps is a bad omen. The robins are a sign of internal imbalance in the hill town. Although they come from elsewhere, they are associated with the return of Sula as a new woman. She is unlike everyone else. She is thirty but looks slim and smart. She is not married like others at a tender age. She dates men but does not get attached to anyone. She shows everybody their shortcomings. It is her presence that sizes up other women and they begin to reorient themselves towards their duties. One free bird is symbolized by the robins. The robins not only dirty the places with their shit, they also die in large numbers. This is a typical magic realist feature. The robins come to live and die along with the inhabitants. Hardly any other pick from nature is integrated in the fabric of the novel. There are the trees and the river but they continue to grow and flow without heed. Only the robins reflect the change in nature. Neither the hills, nor the wind has such a remarkable cffcct on thc lifc of Bottom.

In the death of Chicken Little, the dramatic effect is almost magic realist. It is a piece of reality that is enacted only by the two girls. There is no involvement of the police or the townsfolk or the boy's family. The narrative does not dwell on the search. Rather, the author focuses on the bond of guilt between the girls. It is just one incident that freezes the year 1922. Later when the incident is recalled, the scene in the church assumes greater significance. It is a consolidated sorrow of all the women in the community. The women who wept their hearts out were not crying just for the loss of the boy. They were venting out their private failures.

One of the most remarkable features of this novel is the total absence of White characters. The evil is internal. The suffering is among themselves and the only blame they can find is in sleeping with Whites. When they have to term Sula as evil, they assume that she slept with Whites in the cities. This is psychological segregation that a African American writer reveals to the world. The book identifies the African American American perspectives. In what happens to be a fictional story of a particular community of free African Americans, a critic's interest in the destiny of slaves and African American women gives it a Black feminist reading, such as in a book by Barbara Smith.

Most of the characters in the novel are indeed mothers and girls. The only significant male characters are Ajax and Shadrock and both of them are practically rootless. Shadrock is psychotic and Ajax is unidentified. Ajax was basically A. Jacks, or more precisely Albert Jacks (134). No one knows him. The historicity of the novel is not established by the males. It is the life of the females such as Eva's determination to raise her children, Hannah's housework, Helene's distancing herself from the life of prostitution and Nel's married life that make up the story. In the end, Nel is a charwoman, working hard to raise her three children.

Shadrock and Jude are two African American men who are shattered by the work they do. They represent the common lot of the African Americans but not as slaves. Jude, in particular, is associated to some extent with the lot of labourers. They are promised work but are discriminated against. The death of many African American workers in the tunnel is a historic event that erases the life of the settlement at Bottom. In this way the disappearance of the men seal the fate of the women in the African American community. Like Nel, the women work as servants to continue living. Morrison often refers to the community as one where no one effects a definite change to remove evil. Evil is a part of God and they try to endure it, outlive it but do not organize themselves to remove it:

> In spite of their fear, they reacted to an oppressive oddity, or what they called evil days, with an acceptance that bordered on welcome. Such evil must be avoided, they felt, and precautions must naturally be taken to protect themselves from it. But they let it run its course, fulfill itself, and never invented ways either to alter it, to annihilate it or to prevent it happening again. (Morrison, Sula 90)

In the above lines we note Morrison's universal appeal—the plot of the novel amply illustrates the universality of experience through its magical realist overture.

## Works Cited

García Márquez, Gabriel: 1967, *One Hundred Years of Solitude,* 2003 translated by Gregory Rabassa, HarperCollins, 1970.

Morrison, Toni: *Sula,* Vintage International 2004. eBook

Morrison, Toni: *Beloved,* Plume Books 1989. eBook

Rich, Adrienne. "Contemporary Heterosexuality and Lesbian Existence." *Signs: Journal of Women in Culture and Society* 5, 1980, pp. 631-60.

Smith, Barbara. *Towards a Black Feminist Criticism.* Out & Out Books, 1982.

SECTION FIVE

# PAIN, PLEASURE AND EXISTENTIALISM

CHAPTER 13

# Existentialism in *The Bluest Eye* and Alice Walker's *Meridian*

Vijay Songire

EXISTENTIALISM IS a theory which studies human predicament and the problem of human existence. It is associated with several $19^{th}$ and $20^{th}$ century philosophers who focused on the condition of humans in the universe. Soren Kirkegaard is generally considered the first existentialist philosopher though he did not use this term. He conveyed that individuals are solely responsible for their own life. The main idea of existentialism was developed by Jean-Paul Sartre during World War II under the influence of Dostovosky and Martin Heidegger. Jean-Paul Sartre asserts the existence of humans as, "Man is not only that which he conceives himself to be, but that which he wills himself to be, and since he conceives of himself only after he exists, just as he wills himself to be after being thrown into existence, man is nothing other than what he makes of himself" (29).

Existentialists believe that people have freedom of choice. No external forces are responsible for their actions. Moreover, they show how people struggle hard for achievements. However, the purpose of finding stability and peace of mind is out of their reach. Finally, human beings find no meaning in their life. Therefore, existentialists initially insist that one should have a social as well as political cause to avoid meaninglessness and feelings of alienation.

Existentialism finds its expression in the works of African American writers like Toni Morrison, Richard Wright and Alice Walker. Toni Morrison's *The Bluest Eye* and Alice Walker's *Meridian* truly depict existential sufferings and helplessness of the characters. Both the novels offer an authentic picture of human dilemma of struggle for survival. Sometimes by external forces and many times due to personal decisions the characters suffer the problem of existence and alienation which are the key features of existentialism.

*The Bluest Eye* is an ultimate product of age-old racism in African American society where Morrison makes an attempt to condemn this practice. "Through her fictional enterprise, *The Bluest Eye*, Morrison has attempted an authentic reality of the complex Black and female experience in predominantly White America and she underscores their psychological oppression" (Devika Rani 40).

Morrison strongly believes that racial politics has devalued the African American generations for hundreds of years. The novel offers a realistic picture of three African families i.e., Breedloves, Peals and Louise who fall victims to the racist ideology and follow the ways of the Whites in order to get close to the mainstream White society. In this attempt some of them like Peals exploit the members of their own community in order to become close to the ruling class. Breedlove family is at the centre of the novel and all incidents in the novel are concerned with this family. Cholly Breedlove, the African

American unemployed youth is portrayed in such a way that it clearly indicates the marginal existence of the African Americans in 1920s. The Breedloves go through the experience of dependency, repression, internal racism and alienation. The African Americans in American society became the victims of age-old ideology of racism which is actually a product of the power structure in society. It shows the struggle between the African Americans and the Whites for existence. The Breedlove family consists of four members, Cholly Breedlove, Pauline Breedlove, their son Sammy and daughter Pecola. They live at Thirty-fifth Street in Lorain, Ohio. The life they lead is not a pleasant one. They only live there because they are poor and are racially different from the ruling classes in America. Morrison writes about their living: "Like a sore tooth that is not content to throb in isolation, but must diffuse its own pain to other parts of the body-making breathing difficult, vision limited, nerves unsettled, so a hated piece of furniture produces a fretful malaise that asserts itself throughout the house and limits the delight of things not related to it" (27). The dominant White culture underrates the African Americans. It is indicative of the lower status of the African Americans in White America. This shows that they are made to live peripheral livings, and so they think that they are ugly. It is this ugliness, which makes their life vulnerable. The relationship between Cholly Breedlove and Mrs Breedlove is not a harmonious one. Because all they have ever known is nothing but rejection. This is the only thing they can offer each other, to their children and themselves. The close study of Pauline and Cholly highlights this element of rejection. At the age of four Cholly was abandoned by his mother on account of poverty. She did not hesitate to place him wrapped in two blankets and one newspaper on a junk heap near the railroad. This terrible reality in his life indicates his marginal existence, while Pauline too has been suffering from her infancy. She had nothing but to take care of the house. Later on they met each other. As Morrison writes: "He [Cholly] seemed to relish her company and even to enjoy her country ways and lack of knowledge about city things." (90)

Pecola Breedlove is told from the day she is born that she is ugly. Her mother Pauline feels superior while taking care of her White employer's children. The image of Shirley Temple symbolizes the superiority of White culture. Pecola uses the cup which has the image of Shirley Temples. It makes her feel important. She even eats Mary Jane candies. "To eat the candy is somehow to eat the eyes, eat Mary Jane. Love Mary Jane. Be Mary Jane" (38). Pecola wants to wash out the ugliness of her color through these attempts. She goes through traumatic experiences throughout the novel. Her encounter with the fifty-two-year-old store-keeper makes her aware about her subordinate place in the society. African American boys too harass her at school. Her encounter with Maureen Peal, is one of the disgusting experiences she faces in her life. Moureen humiliates and attacks Pecola in the words: "I am cute! And you ugly! Black and ugly" (56). Geraldine, a middle-class woman also considers her inferior. Pecola knows that it is her ugliness which made her marginal even in her own community. She is treated as an 'other' not only at her home but also in the society at large. She becomes alienated and lives a futile existence. As Morrison writes:

> "Long hours she sat looking in mirror, trying to discover the secret of ugliness, the ugliness that made her ignored

> and despised at school, by teachers and classmates alike. She was the only member of her class who sat alone at a double desk. (34)

Besides Pecola, all the other African American women in *The Bluest Eye* are oppressed and humiliated on account of their race and gender. Claudia explains the harsh reality about her mother and other women in the community. She says, "Being a minority in both caste and class, we moved about anyway on the hem of life." (11) It shows isolation of African American community in a racist American society. When the novel opens, Pecola is seen living with the MacTeers family because Cholly has put the family outdoors, to live at the margin. Cholly who does not find a place in the society is a victim of the White culture. Cholly's unnatural rape of Pecola is one of the poignant affairs in the novel. To rescue Pecola from the dehumanizing gaze of the White people, Cholly rapes her. His violent act of rape reflects his anger as well as his inability to do anything against White society.

As an African American girl, Pecola is humiliated by the Whites as well as by her own community. She also enjoys no freedom like Sammy, her elder brother. In order to avoid all kinds of humiliation and oppression, Pecola yearns to God daily for blue eyes.

Through the character of Pecola, Morrison portrayed the suppression, devaluation of the African Americans in general and women in particular. The Breedlove family thus represents the pathetic condition of the lower-class African Americans in America, they are extremely poor and ostracized. Patrice Bryce rightly asserts, "The double jeopardy of being both poor and ugly excludes Pecola from sharing in whatever social and economic tidbits that may be offered. Pecola's parents cannot fully comprehend the depth of ostracism and are powerless to change the situation" (39).

*The Bluest Eye* basically focuses on the problem of racism, how African Americans are victimized due to the racial prejudices of high and low, and how they lead a marginal existence. Pauline and Geraldine try to assume their fake identities. In the Breedlove family there is nothing but disintegration. There is no love for each other. The MacTeers on the other hand have a sense of maturity and feeling of genuine love.

Thus, *The Bluest Eye* portrays the tragedy and suffering of African American people through the character of Pecola and the Breedloves as well. It culminates in Pecola's rape scene. Pecola's rape by her own father is the distortion of his love for Pecola. Her mother Pauline wishes to accept the White values but in vain. She is not accepted by the mainstream White culture and remains at the margin of the society. Both Pauline and Pecola humiliated and exploited at home as well as in society lead a marginal existence throughout the novel. The existential issues like exploitation, oppression, struggle for survival, identity crisis is blended together in the novel.

Alice Walker unfolds the reality of thc Civil Rights Movement in America amidst racial and gender discrimination. The male as well as female characters in the novel face humiliation, oppression and marginalization from external agencies like American racism.

Meridian discusses themes such as the Civil Rights Movement, gender discrimination, quest for identity, womanism etc. Besides, it has the theme of optimism too where the female protagonist Meridian Hill stands erect against male hegemony and racism in White dominated America. Being a female child, she is neglected at home. Her mother Mrs Hill does not educate her about sex. During her adolescence she falls in love with a boy Eddie. Due to her ignorance about sex, she faces pregnancy at a very tender age. Meridian represents the life of a girl who is humiliated and neglected on account of her gender. Being a girl child, she is sexually harassed by one White man Dexter as well as by his assistant and she finds herself completely helpless. Her marriage with Eddie too remains unsuccessful on account of the hostile attitude of males towards females. Still Meridian shows courage and does not want to be a victim of patriarchy like her mother Mrs Hill. She wants to create her own identity. Meridian is one of the most optimistic characters in Walker's fictional world who always stands erect against all obstacles in her life.

As Pifer rightly observes, "At age seventeen, Meridian is left on her own to consider what to do with her life and her child's. When Meridian says no to motherhood, she offends and loses her own mother, her family, and her community. She feels guilty for leaving her baby and cannot adequately explain why she must. But by shedding her prescribed 'happy mother' role and standing up for her own needs, Meridian takes the first step towards becoming 'a revolutionary petunia'. She stops living by others' standards, learns to bloom for herself, as she must in order to survive, since her rebellious acts will alienate her from the rest of the society..." (60-61). Meridian finds herself trapped in the cycle of gender oppression. But she is ready to fight against all odds in the society. She emerges as a political activist in the Civil Rights Movement in the novel. Her active participation in the Civil Rights Movement stands her apart from other women who became a revolutionary at the end striving hard for the upliftment of the downtrodden people. She is observed as a brave woman who hopes for the betterment of people. In the very first episode, "The Last Return" the element of optimism is strongly observed in the novel when Meridian faces a tank. As the novelist writes, "Meridian did not look to the right or to the left. She passed the people watching her as if she did not know it was on her account they were there. As she approached the tank the blast of its engine starting sent a cloud of pigeons fluttering…" (7). Meridian sets a new example in the field of African American literature by participating in the Civil Rights Movement. She even accepts the outsider girl like Wile Chile and helps her like a sister. Being a woman, she is a good example of female solidarity. She does not want to limit her role just of her own family. Meridian has crossed all boundaries set by the society. She rejects the limitations of the society and wants to lead an independent life of her own which is awe inspiring. As the narrator writes, "With beads of cake and colored beads and unblemished cigarettes she tempted Wile Chile and finally captured her. She brought her into the campus with a catgut string around her arm" (25). Wile Chile represents a group or a class of people which is neglected by the mainstream culture. Meridian's attempt to rescue Wile Chile from her sufferings is remarkable. Meridian's approach towards life is positive and she inspires people around her. She helps characters like Wile Child, Lynne and Truman. At last, she says to Truman, "Besides all the people who are as alone as I am will one day gather at the river. We will watch the evening sun go down. And in the darkness maybe we will know the truth" (242). She believes in doing something for the community in which she lives. This is her ability to inspire people which makes her unique. The novel shows Meridian's struggle for existence. Besides her other characters like Mrs Hill, Wile Child, Miss Lynne struggle for survival.

Meridian, the White girl Lynne, Truman and Tommy Odds are the victims of racism in *Meridian*. Meridian is seduced by one White man at a very tender age. The man just considers her as an object of his sexual fulfillment. It shows the white men's attitude towards African American women. Lynne, the White girl is also a victim of racism. Her racial discrimination takes the highest toll in the form of rape when the African American man, Tommy Odds rapes her. Tommy Odds' rape shows African Americans' hatred for the Whites. In *Meridian* racial discrimination is handled by Walker with the issue of interracial love affair. Truman and Lynne are the interracial couple and their love affair is not successful due to the rigidity of racial ideology. They both get married and live together but with the influence of one of the African American characters Tommy Odds Truman changes his perception of Lynne and at last, he leaves her. Tommy Odds, one of the victims of racism who lost one leg in a racial assault doesn't like Truman's relationship with the White girl Lynne. The relationship of Truman and Lynne is spoiled due to the racial conflict between the Whites and the Blacks. "Walker explores the effects of the burden of history of growing up in a racist society on the relationship between Black women and men, Black men and White women and Black women and White women in the Civil Rights Movement." (Hendrickson 126) Though Truman and Lynne love each other, their relationship doesn't go longer due to the racist culture in America. Actually, being Black Truman loves Lenny, a White girl. She too loves him and both get married and live together. Tommy Odds has racial hatred in his mind for the Whites. He does not like Truman to even mention her name. He says, "All White people are mother fuckers. I want to see them destroyed I could watch their babies being torn limb from limb and I would not lift a finger. The Bible says to bash out the brains of your enemy's children on the rocks. I understand that shit now." (M 132) The White girl Lynne's rape in the novel is very suggestive. Alice Walker highlights the dangers of racial hegemony that was created by the Whites themselves.

Thus, Breedlove family members Pecola, her mother Pauline and father Cholly in Morrison's *The Bluest Eye* and Meridian, Wile Chile, Truman in Alice Walker's *Meridian* present universal human sufferings. The characters in the respective novels struggle for their survival. They want freedom from oppression and humiliation from the society which is more powerful than them. Undoubtedly, both the writers Morrison and Walker have depicted the existential issues like problems of existence, struggle for survival, alienation and quest for identity in these novels. The attempt of their writing is to reveal reality in the contemporary society. They want to signify the idea of equality, liberty and brotherhood for the well-being of the society.

**Works Cited**

Bryce, Patrice. *The Novels of Toni Morrison: The Search for Self and Place within the Community*. New York: Peter Lang, 1992.

Pifer Lynn. "Coming to Voice in Alice Walker's *Meridian*: Speaking out for the Revolution." *African American Review*, vol. 26, no. 1, 1992.

Rani, Devika. *Image of the Women in the Novels of Toni Morrison*. Creative Books: New Delhi, 2008.

Roberta, Hendrickson M. "Remembering the Dream: Alice Walker's *Meridian* and the Civil Rights Movement." *MELUS*, vol. 24, 2 March 2007.

Sartre, Jean-Paul. *Existentialism is Humanism*. London: Methuen & Co., 2007.

Walker Alice. *Meridian*. Harcourt Brace Jovanovich: USA, 1976.

CHAPTER 14

# Feminine Social Revolution: A Study of *Beloved*

Aya Somrani

IN THE 21[st] century, women novelists pioneered a revolutionary activist step forward. Such works gave way to women voices to be recognized among patriarchal societies. Several novels written by women on women occupied an influential position in the world of literature. They have been instrumental in furthering the communal thought through metamorphosis. Feminist works of fiction have given women an occasional chance to call for their rights in their own ways. They are able to put up a fight against the conventional social norms which kill their freedom and bury their identities.

Of all great women narratives, Toni Morrison's *Beloved* is a significantly stimulating work of art. Set in 1873 American Rcconstruction rural Ohio, the novel narrates the story of a former slave woman, Sethe who kills her daughter to save her from a future of slavery. After the daughter's death, she engages in a sexual relationship with a mason to have a tombstone for her daughter's grave, on which she had engraved 'Beloved', which is also the title of the novel.

The opening chapter sets the tone for the whole novel. In this chapter, the African American writer unveils a mysterious ghost who disturbs the peace of Sethe's home, which is although now free of slavery but is still overburdened with its devastating memories and heartbreaking tears. Through flashbacks and fragmented memories, it is discovered later that the feared ghost is Sethe's daughter killed as an infant. The child's absence is encoded in the house's name 124 Bluestone Road, which lacks the number 3, the daughter's position among her brothers as the third child.

The girl's spectrum urges the thirteen years old brothers, Buglar and Howard, to flee the house after horrible encounters with her. Baby Suggs, who has rented the house, dies after the boys' departure. The event has no impact over Baby Suggs, who cannot even remember her first born after she lost her children long ago. Then we have Paul D, the last of the Sweet Home men, who turns up at Sethe's residence. Paul D is also a former slave with Sethe in Sweet Home, Kentucky plantation, ruled by the brutal Schoolteacher, before they escape. As for Denver, Beloved's sister, she lives under the shadow of Sethe's dark memories, which has a crucial impact on her life. She is prevented from enjoying life due to her mother's past. Sethe seems afraid of seeing her daughter wading through the same problems that she has herself faced before. For this reason, her attitude is clearly reflected in her deeds. For instance, when Mr Bodwin comes to pick up Denver for work, Sethe attacks him violently, because the scene reminds her of her past when a group of White men come to pick her up for slavery.

The literary tradition in the 19th and 21st centuries has been entirely masculine. It undermines feminine conception in the field of literature. Morrison in *Beloved,* changes this tradition by writing strong women characters. She starts the first book with the description of an interrupted family, where males in the house (Howard and Buglar) escape Bluestone Road, leaving the women (Denver and Sethe) alone against Beloved`s ghost. It is confirmed that the house, and its dwellers, are controlled by a girl—a baby girl actually. This fact in the text changes the masculine rule to a feminine one. Even Sethe's residence in the house and her courage to fight the ghost is an indicator of a woman's abilities in life.

In this case, women become the novel's heroines. They face the malevolent soul with boldness instead of running far, like the boys did: "Sethe and Denver decided to end the persecution by calling forth the ghost that tried them so" (Morrison 4). In the same framework, the initial narrative of the book explores a lot of the mother-child relation. In other words, it explains a woman's deeper heroic feelings as a mother. Here, Sethe sacrifices her body for a man, to be able to afford a tombstone for her dead baby, and write the letters of her child on it: "Ten minutes, he said. You got ten minutes I'll do it for free. Ten minutes for seven letters" (Morrison 156). So, the protagonist rejects slavery by murdering her new born and then offers her body to build her a suitable tomb. The novel highlights the idea that women are far stronger than men and are able to do many risky tasks.

Besides, there is an exprcssion of woman's high affection towards those she holds dear. Sethe confesses her strong love to her deceased baby. When Denver delivers to her the soul's threat saying, "For a baby she throws a powerful spell", the mother replies, "No more powerful than the way I loved her" (Morrison 13). So, even if Beloved's spirit tries to ruin Sethe's peaceful life, the mother still loves her child. She cannot abandon her baby despite its attempts for revenge. Therefore, here the mother's character, shows an unmatchable strength in enduring torture and bear the burden of a guilt's grief. However, Sethe's personality is different from Baby Suggs, who forgets her eight children, and barely remembers her first infant—"My first-born. All I can remember of her is how she loved the burned bottom of bread" (Morrison p. 5).

At this spot, Sethe recalls several incidents, especially her daughter's carnage; a memory that incessantly lives with her. She still wants her infant to appear so that she can explain herself to it:

> She wasn't even two years old when she died. Too little to understand. Too little to talk much even [...] Maybe. But if she'd only come, I could make it clear to her. (Beloved p.5)

Sethe is not as afraid as she is sad. That is why she clings onto the spirit so tightly. Yet, Morrison embodies again this woman's emotional toughness, that males lack in the novel. For example, Paul D's opinion concerning the ghost mirrors his deprivation of the sixth sense that the mother owns. He thinks Beloved is evil—"What kind of evil you got in here?" whereas, Sethe understands the sprite well; "It's not evil, just sad" (Beloved p. 127).

Furthermore, the novelist insists on the masculine misogyny towards African American females. She puts forward the portrait of the Schoolteacher, the White enraged master, as a sadistic grim reaper. She describes his treatment of Sethe as "punched the glittering iron out of Sethe's eyes, leaving two open wells that did not reflect firelight" (Beloved p. 9).

He steals the joy of life from her in a pugnacious way. The Schoolteacher is depicted here, as the symbol of masculine aggressiveness chaining women without mercy.

In the meanwhile, Toni makes fun of men, when she makes an advance about Kentucky's men. She promotes the idea that men cannot live without women, "They were young and so sick with the absence of women they had taken to calves. [...] All in their twenties, minus women, fucking cows, dreaming of rape, thrashing on pallets, rubbing their thighs and waiting for the new girl" (Beloved p. 13).

There is a clear challenge to the masculine community, making it impossible for them to be psychologically balanced when females are gone. This question takes us further into the novel's themes, linked to human issues.

Morrison's work oscillates among a number of issues and subjects. She presents the female from different angles within divergent social streams. First of all, Morrison examines the theme of humans' bestiality and savagery especially related to men. To illustrate, the Schoolteacher's brutal behavior with slaves (whipping and punishing) is rhetorically labeled as, "schoolteacher arrived to put things in order" (Beloved p. 11).

This is his way to rule in the name of the White man. Such episodes recall the White Man's mission in the European society, which is based on the maxim of other races' extermination, to leave space for the Arian race. According to the White race, they are the only race who deserves to live on earth, since they are believed to be more beautiful and more intelligent. So, the rest of the world must obey and abide to exploitation, in the service of the Whites. Hence, the Schoolteacher attempts to tame and domesticate the African Americans, as part of his mission in the American colonies. He starts with whom he considers the weakest, which is women.

Moreover, the issue of identity imposes itself quite readily in the narrative. In the first chapter, Paul D and Sethe portray Sweet Home merely as a place to live, not as a motherland to cherish, "It wasn't sweet and it sure wasn't home. [...] But it's where we were" (Beloved p. 16). The characters in this case, feel their identities being chattered. They do not even have a home or a land or any belongings. In addition, Denver witnesses a state of psychological trauma. As a female teenager, she needs friends around, but she has none, "Nobody speaks to us. Nobody comes by. Boys don't like me. Girls don't either" (Beloved p. 11). For this reason, the girl's character refers to a torn identity, that is denied by others. She feels marginalized and discriminated. Despite having a house to live, she feels lost and wants to leave, "I can't live here. I don't know where to go or what to do, but I can't live here" (Beloved p. 11). However, it is clear that Denver doesn't have another shelter. In this way, neglect and segregation erase Denver's personality as a female due to her conditions, making her feel deprived from normal life. As Paul D puts it, "It's hard for a young girl living in a haunted house. That can't be easy" (Beloved p. 17).

Sethe resists Denver's desire to leave, and decides to stay in the house. She clings to what she feels is her home, showing a lot of strength once again, "No more running; from nothing. I will never run from another thing on this earth" (Beloved p. 9). Through her delivery, Sethe settles according to her own norms in life. She aims at building her own reality in her own way. The family's lifestyle, as introduced by Morrison in the

19th century, echoes the system of existence in Ohio at that time. The African American women have been physically and psychologically destroyed. There is no cohabitation between the Black and White races. People live in sects. In fact, the African Americans are not treated as humans either. Despite this, the heroine in the novel resists all conditions to prove her existence and change her fate.

Likewise, in order to convey her message concerning women's freedom and rights, Morrison resorts to special narrative techniques. First of all, she mixes the use of language, oscillating between the standard speech and the spoken or slang dialect. Secondly, she fuses the past and the present by means of disrupted narration and memory abundance. Next, the non-linearity of time and events dominates the novel. For this reason, the American author Margaret Atwood states in her article 'Jaunted by Their Nightmares':

> "Ms. Morrison's versatility and technical and emotional range appear to know no bounds. If there were any doubts about her stature as a pre-eminent American novelist, of her own or any other generation, 'Beloved' will put them to rest. In three words or less, it's a hair-raiser." (p.8)

As an Afro-American writer, Morrison explores the traumatizing legacy of slavery that the African Americans face in USA. She casts light on three generations of slaves—the first is Baby Suggs, a freed woman (her son Hall buys her freedom), the second is Sethe, Suggs' daughter-in-law, an escaping slave and the third is Denver, raised in freedom but blemished by her inheritance. Likewise, the author talks about her novel in her book, *Unspeakable things Unspoken: The Afro-American Presence*, "I want to address ways in which the presence of Afro-American literature and the awareness of its culture both resuscitate the study of literature in the United States, and raise that study's standards" (p. 127). Here, Morrison enlightens her audience with a whole slavery chronicle in the United States at the time of the Civil War. She depicts slavery's effect on three generations of women, who prove that agonizing memories remain deeply engraved in their souls even after gaining freedom. In this case, *Beloved*'s author refers to a constant search for a feminine identity construction. Even the dead baby Beloved reincarnates and comes back home, after her illumination, to fetch her family and origins. However, Beloved's acceptance in the house is an issue of mistaken identity. The girl's stream of consciousness reveals memories of an old soul's past life. She remembers "little hills of dead people" (p. 247), and a dark place with "nothing to breathe down there and no room to move in" till she reaches "the bridge" (p. 87). Perhaps the description allures to the slaves' conditions as they are shipped during slave trade, across the Atlantic Ocean. The African Americans were tossed in dark rooms under the deck, while the ones who died were hipped together in the shape of hills to be thrown in the ocean.

Therefore, Morrison's women, in this novel, are eradicated from their mother country, and wade to build a respectful life in a strange society. The 21st century American society appears to evoke misogyny against African American women, using slavery as a weapon to forbid them from an identity, which is bound to freedom. For instance, the multiple flashbacks in the narrative tell that, without her escape, Sethe wouldn't have dreamt of freedom or even a new life. Women oscillate between the ideas of place and belonging. In the novel, African American women are oppressed by White masculine gender, by a White patriarchal society. As an example, the White schoolteacher whips Sethe and tortures her as her master, till she escapes Kentucky plantation, whereas, Mr Bodwin shows severity to Denver, Sethe's daughter, as her employer. In this way, the same aspects of oppression and inequality are echoed each time in a new shape, but the issue—A question of brutal masculine nature binding women's freedom and subverting her position as an equal human being, especially based on the judgement of the colour of their skin.

In fact, Toni Morrison is born in Ohio during the depression. So, her experiences with racism strengthened her stand on Afro-American identity. She attempts to show that roles and behaviors believed to be appropriate for women in the 21st century, rather entrapped them and limited their opportunities in life. She also wants to break up with the maxim saying that women can only reach fulfillment, in community, as wives or mothers. Toni refuses, in her narrative, the traditional role of women which prevents them from competing with men. The author uses Beloved to promote and represent African American women's interests in the American society, as dual nationality or dual citizens.

In her work Morrison records the wretchedness that Sethe and her family go through during and after the American Civil War. Here, a ghost story intermingles with realistic prose to draw the endured misery of slavery survivors. The scattered sequence of events unveils a physical as well as mental trauma threatening Sethe's family. Slavery causes an everlasting pain lingering in the characters' psychology, preventing them from a normal life. Likewise, the writer addresses the theme of community and family's worth in a woman's life. For instance, Beloved's return on her birthday disturbs the family members and leads to the brothers' escape, but not Sethe. The mother accepts to live side by side with the ghost and share memories with her until the end of the novel, when Beloved decides to go by on her own.

Within this framework, the mother Sethe unceasingly mourns her daughter's loss. As a matter of fact, she kills her out of love, not hatred. The mother doesn't want her baby to feel the same pain of slavery under a White oppressive patriarchal community. Historically speaking, African American women have been exposed to beating as well as forced labor. As Morrison says, "not a house in the country ain't packed to its rafters with some dead negro's grief." On one side, slaves, especially women, have been mistreated to the extreme. On the other side, those who try to run away face harsh punishments. This idea is clearly proved by the Fugitive Slave Law of 1850, issued in the 21st century America, as one of the Supreme Court decisions. The act states that fugitive slaves, including women will be hunted by dogs and returned to their masters. Some come to call it "bloodhound law." Such incidences reflect the high suffering culminating in a sternly destroyed emotional legacy.

In this case, Sethe's emotional mental imbalance, mirrored in her past visions and her present feelings, produce a strong woman. She even attracts Paul D's attention as an admirer. At the novel's end he tells her, "you, your best thing" (p.320). Finally, Morrison surprises the audience that a woman's anguish and affliction is nothing but a step forward to become more powerful. In *Beloved*, Sethe is the prototype of a resistant woman rebelling against society and able to do anything to save her family, and regain her freedom. A woman fighting to build her own identity within a storm of patriarchal community. In other words, Toni seems to tell any man that they are lucky if they have "a woman who is a friend of your mind" (p.319).

Toni Morrison's novel is a worldwide masterpiece which best portrays the feminine social revolution in its bare reality within the world of literature. It challenges and pokes at the masculine norms. The author used her narrative in *Beloved* to challenge the norms set by patriarchal society by articulating a historical chronicle, depicting African Americans slavery. The author chooses a African American female former slave to be her novel's protagonist, and grants her with incredible strength and tough heart in resistance against her past and present fate. Women are privileged in Morrison's work as a clever and brave being who understands ghosts and cohabitates with them, while men cowardly flee from home. Even a baby girl is shown as a dangerous entity who banishes away all males by haunting the house. The novel conveys that women can be strong even in the hardest conditions and preserve her emotional toughness, as well as self-esteem better than men. Sethe kills her daughter out of affection then accepts her ghost's torture for the same reason, too. The heroine Sethe teaches the audience a lesson that females can heal themselves from all traumas. Likewise, human issues of identity crisis and Afro-American traditions expressed within the text refer to the fact that a female's role is crucial as a society rebuilder, focusing on her faculties of adaptation and evolution. Through Beloved, Morrison feeds feminine revolution both in literature and history, crowning women as queen of all times and civilizations.

**Works Cited**

Atwood, Margaret. "Jaunted by their Nightmares." *The New York Times*, September 13, 1987.

"Fugitive Slave Act of 1850." https://en.wikipedia.org/wiki/Fugitive_Slave_Act_of_1850. Accessed 16 September, 2016.

Morrison Toni, *Beloved.* Vintage Books: first ed. 1987.

Morrison Toni, *Unspeakable things Unspoken: The Afro-American Presence in Literature*, University of Michigan, 1988.

"The New Canon: the Best in Fiction", reviewed by Ted Gioiahttp://www.thenewcanon.com/beloved.html. Accessed 14 September, 2016.

CHAPTER 15

# Scapegoat for Humiliation and Pain as Depicted in *The Bluest Eye*

Poonam Mor

IN THE world of modern African-American literature, Toni Morrison holds a unique position. In all her writings, Morrison has made an attempt to fairly represent the issues, values, thoughts and opinions of women. Morrison's central focus is to illustrate a feminine form of experience, or "subjectivity," in terms of how one thinks, feels, values, and perceives oneself and the outside world. Morrison's journey focused on the search for self-identity of her female protagonists which began with the sequential arrangement of the psychological traumas which her protagonists experienced. At the conclusion of her works, there is reconciliation, compromise, and impotent resignation but no consolation. Morrison does a fantastic job of capturing the underlying rage of women and their growing sense of liberation and empowerment. She reveals to readers the subliminal symbols of the female brain.

Toni Morrison explores as well as explains the problem of establishing self-worth in a society where the African Americans are victims not only of racism and sexism but of classism also. She also laments the lack of spontaneity and love in the lives of the poor African Americans because of their forced subjugation by White masters. Though love is one of the most important elements in human life as well as necessary component yet it is missing from the lives of African Americans.

The underprivileged African Americans think that being African American makes them inferior and ugly. In a sense, African American individuals of both sexes have internalised White supremacy ideals in addition to accepting them. Because they were once slaves, they were compelled to live only in a state of powerlessness. This occurs throughout *The Bluest Eye* with eleven-year-old Pecola Breedlove. The contrast between her life and the idealised images of beauty and gentility propagated by the predominately White culture actually drives her insane. Her parents use her as a scapegoat for their suffering and shame. She bears the blame for her parents' feelings of shame and guilt from their individual upbringings.

The novel illustrates the catastrophic possibilities of beauty standards which is concerned with people's outward appearance more than their inner values. Such a desire to fit into the socially conventional notion of beauty is best summed up by Patrick Bryce Bjork's comment: "White beauty, White living, White freedom–these are what the characters in *The Bluest Eye* long for, strive for, and yet can never realize" (52).

The racism and inter-racial tensions are what gives Pecola's trauma its poignancy. Both the values of light-skinned Maureen Peal, whose sense of superiority is connected to her hue, and the white beauty standards, which deny Pecola a positive sense of self, are harmful. Pecola doesn't fit the mold, unlike Maureen Peal, her "high yellow dream child" (*BE* 47) classmate. Maureen Peal's actions illustrate that African American children are taught to assume superiority based on the lightness of their skin. She humiliates Pecola by saying, "I am cute! And you ugly! Black and ugly black e mos. I am cute" (*BE* 56). While Pecola, who has dark skin, is viewed as Black, messy, and most importantly, irrelevant, Maureen, who has a fair complexion and striking green eyes, receives preferential treatment from teachers and peers. She internalises the harsh rejection she has experienced from both the White and her own community. Pecola, Claudia, and Frieda experience constant bullying at school from both "Black" and "White" classmates, whereas Maureen is respected and envied. When Pecola falls prey to the norm imposed by an American society that associates beauty with a particular image of the White women, she suffers both physically and mentally. The brown skin and eyes of Pecola have no place in such an arrangement when Pecola is surrounded and teased by a bunch of boys. They make fun of her family and call her names. They harass poor Pecola out of their own contempt for themselves. They are forced to vent their frustrations on her because they are struggling with their own ugly and dark nature. They mock and torture Pecola to make her feel inferior than them, which strokes their egos and pride. She is used as an alibi for their suffering and shame. But all that amounts to an admission of their own identity-related insecurities. The tendency of Black individuals to harass members of their own race is due to self-hatred that is brought on by White hegemony, "The whiteness she [Morrison] castigates represents the dehumanizing cultural values of a society given over to profit, possession, and dominance." (Otten 96).

Cholly Breedlove and Pauline, who are members of the Breedlove family which is a commune of individuals living under the same roof, fight continuously with a terrible fury.

The Breedlove family is compelled to lead an unnatural life by the racial and class-conscious society in which they live. Both White people and Black people undervalue the members of the Breedlove family. They have completely accepted an image of their selves which portray them as ugly. Of course, their "all-knowing master" is a dominant culture that has subtly forced the stereotypes that were created by White men on them. As Claudia explains:

> The master had said, "You are ugly people". They had looked about themselves and saw nothing to contradict the statement; saw, in fact, support for it leaning at them from every billboard, every movie, every glance. "Yes", they had said "You are right". And they took the ugliness in their hands, threw it as a mantle over them, and went about the world with it. (Morrison 28)

Pecola's discontent with her identity, her surroundings, and her need for herself are all manifested in her wish for blue eyes. Pecola actually desires to be white in addition to having blue eyes. This is where her psychic problem began. She thinks that having blue eyes will change her life's miserable circumstances and make her beautiful, likable, and admirable. Teachers will smile, kids will stop making fun of her, shopkeepers will be kind, and her parents will be kind. Morrison rightly points out, "When the strength of race depends on its beauty, when the focus is on how one looks as opposed to what one is, we are in trouble" (88). Therefore, Pecola is in perpetual trouble. However, by no means can she succeed in getting blue eyes and becoming white.

She endures the same humiliation at home. Because her

family members were supposed to be her supporters, she finds that insult unbearable, "Long hours she sat looking in the mirror, trying to discover the secret of the ugliness, the ugliness that made her ignored or despised at school, by teachers and classmates alike" (Morrison 45). She has been made to believe by the world that she is ugly and that blue eyes are a prerequisite for beauty. She so fervently prays every night that she may awaken with blue eyes.

Equally important is the psychological and physical abuse meted out to Black children by their parents, who are also unsure of who they are and are compelled to follow a path of self-destruction, as was the case with Breedloves. They are still unable to provide the supportive environment a youngster needs to flourish and form a healthy sense of self. The main connections and life rituals have been distorted, which has caused a great deal of suffering for Cholly, Pecola's father. Calvin Hernton sees a classic response in some Black male-female relationships, "Blackmen who are themselves victims of oppression [victimize] Black women with what looks like the same oppression" (17). Cholly makes the decision to locate his father in order to discover himself. His father has been the subject of a protracted quest that comes to a terrible end. However, Samson Fuller, his father, seemed more eager to play dice than to embrace his kid. Any chance for him to mature emotionally is overshadowed by his clumsy response to his father's enraged criticisms, which leaves him powerless. He had very few emotional resources growing up. When Cholly realises that nothing attracted him any longer, the process of emotional isolation with his marriage to Pauline is finished. Cholly turns to booze as an adult to quell his fury and frustration. His sadistic romantic behaviour as well as the brutality and violence in his home life are signs of his lifelessness. He cannot be expected to act the family man's part. He lacks the knowledge necessary to raise his kids in a loving setting. Cholly wants to adore Pecola, but her feelings of passion prevent her from doing so. He is completely perplexed, as it is said in the novel:

> His mouth trembled at the firm sweetness of the flesh. He closed his eyes, biting his fingers to dig into her waist. The rigidness of her shocked body, the silence of her stunned throat, was better than Pauline's easy laughter had been. The confused mixture of his memories of Pauline and doing of a wild and forbidden thing excited him.... He wanted to fuck her—tenderly. (Morrison 128)

With this final act Cholly lost all humanity conceivable. Pecola's only response to her father's act is the "... hollow suck of air in the back of her throat. Like the rapid loss of air from a circus balloon," (Morrison 128) suggesting the vacuum Cholly leaves behind. The ultimate kind of parent betrayal and brutality against his daughter is the rape. Cholly's activities turn his kids into unhappy people with a sick, wrapped psycho instead of giving them a home where they can develop into secure, self-assured adults with a sense of self-worth. Pauline, like her husband, lacks emotional bonds and harbours resentment towards Black people in general and her own family in particular. Pauline sees her family as a potential barrier to her happiness and, by extension, the happiness of her White master. Her mother doesn't offer her kids any affection because it might interfere with more crucial matters. The most crucial factor for a young girl's self-esteem to develop is her mother's affection. Pecola, though, is unable to imagine having any self-esteem. Particularly upsetting is her parents' emptiness in life and their intense self-hatred. They are already marginalised by their socioeconomic condition as poor Black people, but their self-perception as ugly isolates them even more and shows self-hatred. The most damaging aspect of their life is their self-hatred. These marginalised Black people are making some effort to adopt white characteristics.

However, the process of adopting white characteristics have its own share of issues. Due to their traumatic life experiences, they feel inferior and want to be someone else. As a result of which, ties between the individual, Pecola, and the African-American community become complicated. She is ultimately shunned, marginalized, and tormented by them.

Thus, Morrison demonstrates how Black people have been alienated from themselves as a result of internalising White beliefs. This narrative presents challenges and tribulations while being straightforward and rife with emotion. It is convincing and compassionate. Pauline, Cholly, Geraldine, Pecola, and the majority of the Black students at school are underprivileged African-Americans who turn to self-hatred as a means of survival. The bigotry and apathy of society have defeated Pecola's family. All members of the African-American community have experienced prejudice and rejection from White culture in varied degrees. The idea that White society is superior has been accepted by Black people. To live peacefully in America, they are completely incapable of creating a healthy atmosphere for themselves. They are all making unsuccessful attempts to bridge the gap between appearance and substance.

## Works Cited

Bjork, Patrick Bryce. *The Novels of Toni Morrison: The Search for Self and Place Within the Community.* New York: Peter Lang, 1992.

Grewal, Gurleen. *Circles of Sorrow, Lines of Struggle: The Novels of Toni Morrison.* Baton Rouge: Louisiana State University Press, 1998.

Hernton, Calvin. *The Sexual Mountain and Black Women Writers.* New York: Anchor–Doubleday, 1987.

Klotman, Phyllis R. "Dick-and-Jane and the Shirley Temple Sensibility in *The Bluest Eye.*" *Black American Literature Forum* 13, Sept. 1979, pp. 123-25.

Morrison, Toni. *The Bluest Eye.* New York: Holt, Rinehart and Winston, 1970.

Otten, Terry. *The Crime of Innocence in the Fiction of Toni Morrison.* Columbia: University of Missouri Press, 1989.

Samuels, Wilfred D., and Clenora Hudson–Weems. *Toni Morrison.* Boston: Twayne Publishers, 1990.

Weever, Jacqueline de. "The Inverted World of Toni Morrison's *The Bluest Eye* and *Sula.*" *CLA Journal*, vol. 22, 1979, pp. 402-14.

# CONTRIBUTORS

**1. Dokubo Melford Goodhead** (PhD) is a graduate from the University of Nigeria and the University of Washington. He taught at Spelman College and was the Associate Director of the 'African Diaspora and the World Program' there. His scholarly articles have appeared in the journals *Folklore, Legon Journal of the Humanities*, and the *Contemporary Journal of African Studies.*

**2. Lehasa Moloi** (PhD) is a Lecturer in the Department of Development Studies at the University of South Africa. He holds Master's Degree in Development Studies. He is a Doctoral student addressing the topic: Towards an Afrocentric Development Paradigm in Africa. He is passionate about Decolonization debates, most particularly, pursuing scholarship in Afrocentricity as an African-centered decolonial paradigm.

**3. Abdelkader Ben Rhit** (PhD) is an Assistant Professor of English Language and Literature at Gabes University, Tunisia. Interested in postcolonial writings, he has published papers on Ben Okri, Toni

Morrison, Joseph Conrad, E.M. Forster and Shakespeare in national and international peer reviewed journals and presented these at national and international conferences.

**4. Bhawana Pokharel** (PhD) is an Assistant Professor of English at Prithvi Narayan Campus, Pokhara. A DANIDA MPhil and PhD Scholar in Migration and Diaspora Writings, from TU Nepal and Aarhus University Denmark, her work in the academic front essentially straddles the broader spectrum of Human Rights and Justice in both literary and cultural discourses. Her book *Human Rights: Concepts, Confusions and Clarifications* (2018) showcases her inquiry into this field. She has numerous academic publications from home and abroad. She is also a creative writer. Her creative space charters her deeper personal musings combined with socio-political observations as evident in her anthologies *Casolate* (2015) and *Midnight Muse* (2018). Alongside, she lends a fervent voice to women empowerment and gender equality through articles in periodicals, and media interviews.

**5. Tamara Miles** (EdD) teaches English in a college in South Carolina. She is a former administrator of *The Curiosity Salon* and the host of an audio literary journal called 'Where the Most Light Falls,' at SpiritPlantsRadio.com. She was a contributor at Sewanee Writers' Conference, 2016 and a resident at Rivendell Writers Colony, 2017.

**6. Saikat Sarkar** (PhD) is an Assistant Professor in the PG Deptartment of English, Midnapore College (Autonomous). Before this he was a tenured faculty at the PG Dept of English, Bankura Christian College. His doctoral dissertation was on the cultural influence of the *Bible* on the novels of Toni Morrison. A recipient of US Department of State fellowship, Dr Sarkar has participated in NEH Summer workshop in Rochester, NY in 2011. He has published twelve research articles and eight book chapters on Black American Literature, Black British Literature, Popular Culture, Indian Partition and Indian English Drama in national journals and edited volumes. Dr Sarkar is actively engaged in translation projects. Prominent among these are the ones on tribal folk literature, partition narratives and Indian English poetry in anthologies. Dr Sarkar has edited noted academic research journals named *Wesleyan Journal of Research* (a multi-disciplinary peer-reviewed journal) and *Appropriations* (a peer-reviewed national-level journal of English literary studies) and has been acting as reviewer for peer-reviewed national-level journals like *Post-Scriptum* and *Post-Colonial Interventions.*

**7. C. Raju** (PhD) is an Associate Professor and Head, Department of English, Yadava College (Autonomous), Madurai, Tamil Nadu. He has 28 years of teaching experience both at the UG and PG Levels. He has presented and published numerous papers in various Seminars, Conferences, Journals and Anthologies. Under his guidance eight scholars have been awarded doctorate and six others are pursuing their research. He is an Examiner in many universities for evaluating PhD Thesis and for conducting Viva voce. His area of interest is Indian Writing in English, Diasporic Literature and American Fiction.

**8. Cyrine Kortas** (PhD) is an assistant teacher of English Language and Literature in the Higher Institute of Languages, Gabes Tunisia. In 2018, she defended her PhD thesis in comparative literature, entitled 'Voices of Disobedience: Redefining Femininity in Edith Wharton's and D. H. Lawrence's New Woman Fiction.' Her areas of interest are gender and feminist studies, race and religious studies. She has been participating in a number of international conferences both at home and abroad.

**9. Nitesh Narnolia** (PhD) is a Senior Research Fellow at Centre for Diaspora Studies, Central University of Gujarat, Gandhinagar. Author, Editor and Reviewer, his research interest includes Transnationalism, Diasporic Literature, Slave narratives, Afro-American Literature, Postcolonial and Subaltern Studies, Race and Ethnic Studies and Film Studies. He has presented 30+ research papers in International/National conferences/seminars and has around 15 research articles published in different journals, books and research monographs. He is the co-editor of *Identity, Diaspora and Literature: Theorising New Diasporic Consciousness* published in 2018. His another book, entitled *Exploring Identity in Transnational Space: A Critical Study of Meera Syal's* Novel and Films was published in 2019. He has received full fellowship to attend a 15-days symposium, Brown International Advance Research Institute 2018 (BIARI 2018) at Brown University, RI, USA. He is one of the reviewers of DJ Journal of English Language and Literature and Journal of National Institute of African Studies, London. He is also a part of the Editorial Board of Newsletter and Journal of Global Research Forum on Diaspora and Transnationalism (GRFDT), New Delhi.

**10. Sneha Sawai** (PhD) is Assistant Professor of English at Kalindi College, Delhi. She is working on African-American Literature from IGNOU under the guidance of Professor Nandini Sahu. Her areas of interest are: American Literature, Women's Writing and Popular Literature.

**11. Dipankar Parui** (PhD) is an Assistant Professor of English in Hijli College, Kharagpur, West Bengal. He has a Doctoral Degree from the Department of English and Culture Studies, The University of Burdwan, West Bengal for his dissertation on Rohinton Mistry's Fiction. He has authored three books: *Anxiety of Parsi Minority: A Study of Rohinton Mistry's Short Stories, Locating the Minority Voices in Rohintom Mistry's Novels* and *Selected American Short Stories: Poe Fitzgerald Faulkner.* The areas which stimulate his academic and research interest to Dr Parui are Parsi English Literature, Diaspora Studies, Postcolonial Literature, New Literature, Indian English Literature, English language Teaching and Phonetics.

**12. Anuradha Bhattacharyya** (PhD) is author of four books of poetry, four novels, two academic books, over 150 poems published in anthologies and journals and 23 short stories published from Georgia, Texas, England, Kenya, New Delhi, Chandigarh, Tamil Nadu, Andhra Pradesh, Kerala, Madhya Pradesh and West Bengal. She has received the Best Book of the Year (2016) Award from Chandigarh Sahitya Akademi for her English novel *One Word,* Best Book of the Year (2019) Award for *Still She Cried* and a book-grant to publish her collection of poems *My Dadu* dedicated to her grandfather Sri Asoke Kumar Bhattacharyya, Padma Shri, 2017. She has received the Poiesis Award for Excellence in Literature from Poiesis International in a Short Story Contest, Bengaluru, 2018. Her story was titled *Painting Black and Blue.* She has been honoured with Sahitya Shree from Kafla International at Udaipur, 2016. She was Guest of Honour at World Peace Thinkers and Writers Meet,

Kolkata, 2015 and 2019. She was honoured as Distinguished Poet by the President of the Zila Parishad at Amaravati Poetic Prism, Vijayawada, 2017, 2019 organised by the Cultural Centre of Vijayawada and Amaravati (CCVA). She was a Distinguished Poet in Haridwar Literature Festival, 2018. Besides creative writing, she has written scholarly articles on her topics of interest, psychoanalysis and Buddhism. Chandigarh Administration has awarded her the Commendation Award for her work in the field of Art & Culture on Republic Day of India, 2019.

**13. Vijay Songire** (PhD) is working with St. John College of Humanities and Sciences, Palghar, Maharashtra. He has completed his M.Phil (2008) as well as PhD (2017) in English literature from North Maharashtra University, Jalgaon. His interest lies in African American literature, Indian Writing in English as well as Communication Skills. Moreover, he has more than 52 papers published with National and International Journals. He has participated as well as presented papers at International conferences too.

**14. Aya Somrani** is a Tunisian University teacher in English language and literature. She has a Master's Degree in English literature in the field of Shakespearean drama from Manouba University in Tunisia. She has taught in two Tunisian universities for two years before she started teaching in Saudi Arabian university of Northern Borders, four years ago. She has published a couple of novellas in English: *The Book of Cyrus* under the pen name Aya Somrani, and *A Demon's Prophecy* under the pen name of Anne Eugene.

**15. Poonam Mor** (PhD) is an Assistant Professor in the Department of Languages and Haryanvi Culture, College of Basic Sciences & Humanities, CCS Haryana Agricultural University, Hisar, Haryana. Her area of interest in research includes Feminism and Postcolonial Studies.